NEVER QUIT ON A BAD DAY™

Inspiring Stories of Resilience

Inspiring Stories of Resilience

PHEBE TROTMAN
& Accomplished Athletes

PUBLISHED BY PHEBE TROTMAN

Never Quit on a Bad Day™
Inspiring Stories of Resilience
Phebe Trotman & Accomplished Athletes

Cover Design & Layout by Margaret Cogswell Designs

Ordering Information:
Special discounts are available on large quantity purchases.
For details: please contact hello@neverquitonabadday.com

May you always know and believe in the
champion you were born to be.

TABLE OF CONTENTS

FOREWORD

By Carl Valentine

Canada Soccer Hall of Fame Honoured Member,
Retired Professional Soccer Player and Coach

In life, we are all confronted with moments that test our resolve, challenge our perseverance, and push us to our limits. It's during these times we often find ourselves questioning whether to press on or to throw in the towel; the decision to persist or to quit becomes our defining moment.

I consider myself lucky to have the professional soccer career I had. Though I'm now retired, currently I am the Club Ambassador for the Vancouver Whitecaps Football Club. During my career I played for teams in England, Canada, and the United States, winning the North American Soccer League with the Vancouver Whitecaps in 1979, four consecutive Canadian championships with the Vancouver 86ers team, and I also played on the 1986 Canadian World Cup team. I got to play in front of big crowds, travel the world, and meet many great people like Phebe Trotman. I first met Phebe over 20 years ago when she played on the Vancouver Whitecaps women's team. She was a fantastic soccer player but an even better person who always has a positive attitude. So I

wasn't surprised to see her become a very successful coach.

Phebe is the perfect person to write this book. I'm sure she has had a few bad days; however, you would never know it when you are around her. Sports in many ways mirrors life, and many athletes will tell you that "You find out what you're made of, not in the good times but through the adversity you overcome."

At the start, I mentioned many of my accomplishments throughout my career, but it was not all great, especially in my early days. Growing up in England, I was kicking a ball as soon as I could walk, and like many other young players, my dream was to become a professional soccer player. As a kid, I played on many teams representing Manchester boys and I was one of the top prospects for my age. At 16, I was invited for a tryout with a club called Stockport County, along with two of my school classmates. This was my chance to make my dreams come true. We were there for six weeks, and I thought we all played really well. We were pulled into the coach's office one at a time, and to my disappointment, I was let go, while my two mates signed professional contracts.

I had been waiting for this chance as long as I could remember, and I was not sure I would get another chance. My mom and dad sat me down and told me I needed to further my education because soccer might not be in the cards for me, and I needed something else to fall back on. They suggested I do that and also keep playing soccer for the school and youth clubs and see what happens. It was not something I wanted to hear, but I had one of the most rewarding experiences that has stuck with me for the rest of my life. I was not the best student in school. I was someone who did just enough to get by. Taking my parents advice, that year I got A's in all my studies and was on my way to university to become a physical education teacher. I knuckled down, worked hard, and even though it was not my dream, I showed myself with hard work and believing in myself, I could accomplish anything.

I still continued to train hard on the field and the next summer, I was invited to train with a soccer club called Oldham Athletic. After a six-week camp, I signed my first professional contract, and the rest is history.

Now, I'm a club ambassador and I get to go into our community and make a difference. I meet so many great people who donate big money, who champion great causes, and many people who volunteer their time to help families who are less fortunate. Often this does not make the news, which is sad, as we need to hear more uplifting stories and increase the positivity that is around us.

We all need more encouraging stories in our lives and this book is filled with these inspiring stories. Each story in this book is a testament to the power of the human spirit, a reminder that in the face of hardships, we have the strength to endure, to persevere, and to emerge stronger on the other side. With Phebe's

MY INSPIRATION

The Beginning of a Journey

MY INSPIRATION
The Beginning of a Journey

When I first envisioned this book series, I had a plan to finish the first book, *Never Quit on a Bad Day: Inspiring Stories of Resilience —Thriving Entrepreneurs* and start this one as soon as the first one was published. A typical go-getter attitude, right? However, life had other plans. Have you ever laid out a plan that you were so sure about, and it ended up taking a few twists and turns? Yes, me too—and many times!

Yet here we are—we made it. I'm excited for you to dive into this book. It's a compilation of short stories and lessons I wish I had read, learned, and acted upon during my younger days. This is the book I didn't know I needed, yet I really did!

Why do I say that? Because the stories will inspire you, and the lessons contained are applicable to your current circumstances, wherever you currently are. There's a reason you're reading this book right now. Something or someone compelled you to pick it up. I believe this is the book that will help you embrace, navigate, and grow through life's twists and turns.

As mentioned earlier, I had a plan for this book, but life had its own plan, so I had to take a bit of a pause. Truthfully, it has been a struggle to find the mental energy to write and start this next book in the series. Not because I'm not excited about it—because I am genuinely thrilled for how the stories and lessons in this book will help you and others—but because I've felt so stretched personally.

The week after the launch of *Never Quit on a Bad Day: Inspiring Stories of Resilience —Thriving Entrepreneurs*, my mom had an unexpected fall and fractured her patella and collarbone. Along with her starting to show signs of dementia over this past year, it has meant a huge shift, as I am now her primary caregiver. While I'm grateful to be able to care for her during this very challenging time, it has been emotionally very difficult, and it has required a major transition and shift in priorities and organizing my schedule.

Throughout this extended pause and even now, I've had to remind myself daily why I decided to start this book series. Remembering the ultimate goal of this book series, to encourage people to keep going even when there are challenges, has been the fuel needed to start writing and keep going, too. I've had to remind myself of the many lessons shared in the first book, such as finding things and moments to be grateful for, even on challenging days. I've reminded myself that I have gone through (and grown through) tough situations in the past and I can do it again. I've had to focus and visualize the finished "published book" and the people it will help once released. I've had to remind myself of my goals and the commitment I made to myself.

I have been especially excited about this book because of a turning point in my young athletic life, when

I was a completely discouraged Under 14 soccer player. I've often thought of how differently my life may have turned out had I quit. In hindsight, that one experience taught me so much and it set me up to enjoy an incredible athletic career. I've had some exceptional athletic moments. I've been inducted into the Coquitlam Sports Hall of Fame as an athlete, been honored as a team member in the B.C. Sports Hall of Fame and Museum and recognized on two teams in the Burnaby Sports Hall of Fame. I'm listed on the B.C. Soccer Heritage Roll of Honour and

hold several titles such as two-time Master's National Champion, W-League Champion, W-League Player of the Year, Women's Premier League National Champion, British Columbia's Adult Player of the Year, Simon Fraser University Female Athlete of the Year, NAIA Champion, NAIA Championship Finals MVP, NAIA Women's Soccer Player of the Year, two-time First Team All-American, and under-19 National Champion. There have been many highs in my athletic career. Some of my greatest winning moments and life lessons are as a result of participating in sports and some of my closest friends now are former teammates. However, there have also been some significant lows and extremely tough moments on the road to these achievements.

I remember this most challenging day like it was yesterday. A friend of mine and teammate encouraged me to try out for the Provincial Team. I wasn't really familiar with what that even meant, but I thought it would be fun to do it together with a couple of other teammates. Plus, I loved to play, so I was excited at the opportunity to play soccer even more. We had several practices leading up to the tryout tournament, where we would play a couple of games and the group would be cut to a smaller number of players. Then that smaller group would go into another set of training sessions and from there, the final Provincial Team would be decided. I remember the coach who was assigned to our group of players asking what position we played, and I told him I played forward/striker. However, he had it in his mind that I was a defender, so defense it was.

We played two games in the tryout tournament where I played outside defense and I thought I played OK, although I definitely wouldn't say I played well enough to stand out. After the two games they brought all the players in and the head coach of the soon-to-be-formed team shared that he appreciated everyone who came out and he would call out the names of players who would move forward to the next round.

Picture it—you are standing with more than 50 players and a coach is calling out names of those who would move forward. I fully expected to hear my name, as I was one of the top players on my community team. He went through the entire list of names—but he didn't call mine. At first, I thought it was a mistake, because of course I thought I was going to make the team! So, when my name wasn't called, I waited a couple of minutes, expecting the coach to correct himself and say my name. But then he said all the players whose names weren't called can be dismissed so they can discuss next steps. I knew then it wasn't a mistake. I didn't make it to the next round. My friends and teammates all made it to the next round, so I was happy for them and congratulated them. They all gave me that awkward look of, "we don't even know what to say," so I said goodbye and walked away. I think I was still in shock as I walked to my dad, who was waiting in the car, and told him the news.

As soon as the words were out of my mouth, it hit me, and I started to sob. I was so devastated and felt embarrassed and so deflated and disappointed that I didn't even make it past the first round. I cried for a long time. One of my friends who made the first round was also released after the next round of training, and sadly, she didn't make the Provincial Team either. Two of our community team teammates did make the Provincial Team, one very talented player and another teammate who wasn't regarded as one of the stronger players on our team. This hurt even more because many teammates and even parents of teammates were confused and shocked that she made the team, and I didn't. So more tears again, and even more confusion and disappointment. Have you ever had one of those moments where you felt completely deflated and then, as you start to work through those emotions, you get hit with another blow? That's how I felt. I was crushed that I didn't make it and to find out a player who didn't contribute much to our community team made this Provincial team hit hard—more tears again.

My parents finally had enough of me hanging out in the basement on the couch crying because I remember them sitting me down and saying, "What's done is done. The decision has been made." Then they asked me what I wanted to do next.

Do you want to continue to play soccer?

Do you want to quit the sport because of one coach's decision?

It was hard to hear those words, because I didn't think it was fair that I didn't make that team, but my parents reminded me there wasn't anything I could do to change the coach's decision. **They also reminded me I did have the *power to choose how I responded to this situation.*** I have the power to make my own decision about what is next for me with regard to soccer. They encouraged me to focus on what I could control, which was my extra training, my mental toughness, and my attitude.

I continued to work on my own skills with my dad and my brother in our backyard, and most times, on my own, just me and my ball. I worked on my physical strength and fitness in the gym. Looking back on that experience, as tough as it was, it set me up for a great career as an athlete and in life, because it taught me to focus on what *I can control*—my work ethic, my resilience, my focus, my perspective, my commitment, and my attitude. Looking back on that experience, I didn't adjust very well mentally to playing another position and that may have been part of the reason I didn't make the team. Instead of embracing that opportunity and shifting my perspective to see it as potentially a testament to my ability that the coach thought I could play a different position, I let other ideas creep into my head, which probably impacted my performance.

That summer, I made a decision: Whatever team I played on in the future, I was going to be an impact player. I would take advantage of every opportunity I'm given on the field, and that whether it is five minutes or a full 90 minutes or anything in between or more (overtime can happen), I make my presence on the field seen, known, and felt.

It's easy to see awards and championship titles and think I've had a smooth athletic career, but it definitely hasn't been that way. Even though I was recruited to play university soccer, I didn't have a guaranteed starting spot right away, as the team already had a very strong lineup when I joined the team. My first year, there were some games I did start, but the majority of the season, I came into the game off the bench, as a sub. And I made sure when I did come into the game, my presence was felt. I chose to work hard.

My professional career was the same. I chose to:
- have a great attitude and be a team player
- make an impact.
- make the most of every minute on the field I was given
- play to the best of my ability.

It is easy for us to see other people's successes and think it was a straight path to the top. How often do we stop to think that a person we look up to may have gone through a similar challenge to the one we are going through? Maybe the only difference is that they pushed through their challenge to get to where they are right now. Or maybe they are just a little further along in their journey.

This is why I'm so excited for this book series because it shares the story behind the story. **It shares how our setbacks lead to our setups. It shares how our struggles are the stepping stones to our successes. It shares how persevering through our challenges leads to our growth.** And it shares how our perspective and attitude of gratitude will help us find a little more happiness along the way.

Throughout writing this book, there have been many extremely challenging moments. And I've *chosen* to hold on tightly to the words "never quit on a bad day" and to keep moving forward, one step at a time. I've *chosen* to visualize the smiles of the people around the world who will read this book and will stay inspired because of the words and lessons on these pages. I've *chosen* to imagine the people who will read this book and will go after their dreams and the ripple effect they will create that will positively impact their friends, their families and their communities. We all have the power to *choose*, and it is in these *choices* that champions are made!

If you haven't read the first book in this series, *Never Quit on a Bad Day: Inspiring Stories of Resilience—Thriving Entrepreneurs*, I encourage you to get a copy and read it too. There are incredible lessons in that book that will help, encourage, and inspire you to create and live a life you love. I also share in the first book the full story of how, why, and where the idea first started for the *Never Quit on a Bad Day: Inspiring Stories of Resilience* book series.

This book, *Never Quit on a Bad Day: Inspiring Stories of Resilience— Accomplished Athletes*, is filled with a few more stories—stories from talented athletes that I look up to who have inspired me along my journey. It is filled with their stories about a challenging time and why they didn't quit.

I believe in business, in sports, in relationships, and in life, we need to share more of the tough stuff. We need to share about the challenging days and the times we want to quit! We need to start sharing about the frustrating moments and days when we ask ourselves, "Is it even worth it?" More importantly, we need to share what we did (or didn't do) to push through those days. We know all people have tough days. But really, how hard are those days and what, how, and why did they keep going?

Your bad moments, day(s), and seasons will most likely look a little different from the stories you will read in this book and other books in this series, but there will be parallels and life lessons you can learn from every story. Included at the end of every chapter is a section titled "Reflections on Resilience." This segment features a series of reflective questions designed to guide you on your personal growth journey. These exercises will prompt you to reflect on your own experiences and also provide practical tips and lessons to help you stay energized as you pursue your goals and dreams. Be sure to also scan the QR code at the end of every chapter for a short message of encouragement from my incredible contributors, too. My prayer is that you will connect with a lesson or a tip in one of these stories, in the reflection exercises and the videos of encouragement that will help you find, remember, and grow in your resilience and strength so together, we can inspire our friends, our family, our communities to **Never Quit on a Bad Day!**

CHAPTER 1

ECHOES OF EXCELLENCE

Dante Fabbro

ECHOES OF EXCELLENCE

Dante Fabbro

Hockey was a pretty predominant activity in our family. Sports, in general, was a big part of my family's lives and how we grew up. My childhood was great. I was extremely competitive and excelled as a young athlete. My parents, my siblings, and the people around me have played a pivotal role in my life by helping to push me to work hard and meet my goals.

Every summer, the whole family would hang out at our family cottage. We played everything from soccer to board games. It could get very competitive with all the cousins! That environment drove me, and we are still a close family.

Like a lot of young Canadian kids, growing up I looked up to the National Hockey League players, and it was a dream to play there someday. As a child, it can seem so far-fetched, but as you climb through the ranks, start playing and progressing at the higher age groups, you can see the improvement and your goal begins to feel a little closer.

My competitive streak started very early; it's been part of my mindset and how I've approached everything about where I want to be in life.

I started to play hockey when I was very young, and when I say I was young, I was probably only two years old when I first put on some rollerblades out in our driveway. As a child, I would play street hockey for hours. I would play for a couple of hours, go inside, and then go back outside to shoot more pucks. I was obsessed with the sport.

Most of my memories growing up playing hockey are very positive and I still have a lot of great friends from my childhood and teenage years playing.

While I was obsessed with hockey, I played a little lacrosse and a few school sports. Playing different sports is actually great for young athletes, because being athletic and mobile in a lot of areas can help you in your chosen sport. What I learned from playing lacrosse was how to hit and the hand eye coordination with the ball really translated well into hockey. When sports got very competitive and I had to focus on one sport, it was an obvious choice; I chose hockey and made it my career.

My first couple of years, I played at Coquitlam Minor Hockey in my hometown and then switched over to the Burnaby Winter Club (BWC) at 8 years old, where I played until I was about 14. Every other year, from age 9 to 14, I played up an age bracket. When I was 13 years old, our team won the Bantam Western Championship. This is around the age when players start to get scouted for the Canadian Hockey League, and with my draft year the next year, I had to prove myself my first year in the league. When we won, I realized I was getting noticed and getting recognition for my play.

My minor hockey association with the Burnaby Winter Club also played a pivotal role in my journey. I was taught to go into tournaments expecting to dominate. Obviously, when you get to a professional level, you have to adapt your game to the speed and your role, but if you just have the mindset of wanting to dominate the guy next to you or the opposing team, that goes a long way.

After playing at BWC, at age 15, I played one year for the Vancouver Northwest Giants. Then I moved to Penticton and played two seasons in the British Columbia Hockey League.

It wasn't and still isn't always easy. A lot of people don't realize the intense work you have to put in and how difficult this journey can be. Everyone wants to see results immediately, and that doesn't always happen. **But once you've pushed through enough difficult days, you know there's light at the end of the tunnel, even on the days you don't always see that light.** Stick with your process and your goals, be consistent in your routine and mindset, and take it step-by-step. I've had many bad days, but I've come to learn how to switch my brain to, "Let's just go do this and get it over with."

Photo credit: Peter Schatz /
Alamy Stock Photo

More often than not, I come out the other side really happy that I pushed through.

I learned this lesson fairly early, around age 8 or 9, when I had come home from grade school and was faced with dryland training. This is where we worked on strength and conditioning exercises off the ice and off our skates, to increase our strength and explosiveness on the ice. These training sessions were very effective, but brutal. My dad was also doing the dryland training with us to stay in shape. But my friends and I hated this field workout.

So one day I called my dad after school, and said, "Dad, I don't want to go. I'm too tired." And my dad sternly said, "Well, if you don't want to do this, then you can forget about going to hockey later. This is what it's going to take to excel at the next level. If you want to stay where you are, fine, but if you want to set your goals and achieve them, you can't skip out on workouts." Thinking about it now, it's crazy that this is a core memory for me. I was crying, but I remember calling my dad back and saying I'm going to go. This was the first turning point where I realized reaching my dream was not going to be easy. It was a powerful lesson to commit to the process and keep going.

Going through days when you're tired, sick, or you have other things going on in your life, you have to battle the negative self-talk that says, "It's too hard," or, "I'm too tired." You have to work through, even knowing the energy it will cost you. At a young age, I was full of energy and just wanted to go out there and play hard. I could be on the ice for hours on end. But as you get older, your body starts to wear down a little more. So those negative thoughts of, "Why am I doing this? It's too early. I'm too tired, I'm too sore," need to be pushed away more often and I go back to the lesson my dad taught me at that young age.

It can be so easy to be negative or focus on a mistake you made in a game or in life. It's cliché, but the power of positive self-talk goes a long way with your mindset. Being consistent with positive self-talk is one of the hardest things to do. **When you're confident in how hard you've worked, how hard you've trained, that confidence comes into your mindset and becomes part of how you want to approach every day.** Not everyone on your team or around you will be doing their best every day, but if you can be the leader and the voice of positivity, it can really turn things around.

At times when negative self-talk can creep in, I think it's important to take a step back and reflect on your journey. For me, when negative thoughts come, I remember, "There's a reason why you're here, because if you weren't good enough, you wouldn't be here." The team I play with right now does a lot of things together as a team, both at the rink and away from it. We are very positive and use self-talk to our advantage. I've recently started journaling, and it's become a great tool for me. If you have a bad day, you can reflect on it and look back on your journal entries to see what you did on other bad days to get back into a good mindset.

Photo credit: CTK / Alamy Stock Photo

Even though I was set on making it to the NHL, my parents were strict about my schooling, ensuring I got an education, too. Since I'd gone to Penticton to play in the BCHL, I had kept my eligibility to go to the National Collegiate Athletic Association and wanted to pursue school that way. I'd talked with my dad about maybe going to the Canadian Hockey League, but I had a feeling he wanted me to go to school.

It's hard as a 17-year-old kid trying to make a decision that might affect many years of your life. My end goal was to make the NHL, and I eventually felt comfortable that the school route was the best for me. After my second year in Penticton and just having graduated high school, at age 18, I made my way to Boston University, where I played three years. As soon as our season ended my junior year, at age 20, I made it to the NHL and signed with the Nashville Predators. I played my first game about a week later. I've been with the Predators for five seasons, and just signed an extension for one more year. I love the city of Nashville and I've loved playing here.

Photo credit: CTK / Alamy Stock Photo

What makes good memories is how hard the road is and when you finally get there, how great it feels. I just work on controlling the things I can control and don't worry about the things I can't. I am prepared every day and as a high-performance athlete, I'm never satisfied with where I'm at and I always want to continue to be better. That's how my mindset's been my entire life. I think as a young athlete I had an edge over a lot of kids because I've always been extremely competitive, I commit to the process and work really hard, and I love to play hockey and that's probably why I am in the NHL today. I'm appreciative of where I am right now, but it's an ongoing grind and you have to find ways to excel. For me, the biggest hurdle is figuring out new ways to explore my game and continuing to improve every day.

Being a professional athlete encompasses many different aspects of life, including nutrition, sleep, taking care of yourself away from the rink, showing up to the rink, and playing. I've had a lot of learning curves and right now I feel I'm in the best place I've ever been mentally. I've definitely grown a lot since I've turned pro, and I want to continue to push my potential and be the best version of myself, both personally and as a professional hockey player.

ABOUT DANTE FABBRO

Dante Fabbro first strapped on rollerblades at the age of 2. Now 25, he is a highly regarded professional hockey defenseman, achieving a childhood dream. Dante represented Canada at the World Junior Championships, where the team won gold in 2018. He also contributed to the team's silver medal at the 2019 IIHF World Championship. Drafted 17th overall by the Nashville Predators in the 2016 NHL Entry Draft, he chose to retain his NCAA eligibility and played for the Penticton Vees of the British Columbia Hockey League, where he was named top defenseman. From there, Dante went to Boston University, where he was a standout player and team co-captain, playing 111 games and posting 80 points, the most among any team defenseman in that time period. Dante joined the Nashville Predators in 2019, where he quickly proved his skill on the ice.

Take a look at Dante's motivating video message on chasing your goals and dreams!

REFLECTIONS ON RESILIENCE

Did you know that a significant portion of our self-talk consists of negative thoughts? Some studies suggest that of the thousands of thoughts we have each day, the majority of them are negative. This highlights the importance for a shift in our internal dialogue.

In Dante's story, he shares the impact that positive self-talk has on achieving our goals and dreams. Dante learned how to turn his self-talk from "I'm too tired" to "let's just go do this" focusing on achieving his dream of playing in the NHL. He knew making it to the NHL would require hard work and committing to the fundamentals even on days when he didn't *feel* like it. By pushing through on those tough days, more often than not, he would come out happy that he did it.

In Chapter Two of *Never Quit on a Bad Day: Inspiring Stories of Resilience—Thriving Entrepreneurs*, we review the difference between success language and limiting language in the Reflections on Resilience section and how our language can either set us up for success or hold us back. Even a small change in our language and self-talk from "I have to" to "I get to" or "I choose to" can positively impact our attitude. It is important we are intentional about the language we use when speaking to ourselves and also with others.

Retraining our minds to embrace positivity is a gradual and continual process. In a world often filled with negativity, cultivating optimistic thoughts requires conscious effort and practice.

Consider this: Would you speak to your younger self or a loved young child in the same manner as you speak to yourself at times? Take a minute and simmer on that question.

Picture a toddler taking their first steps. Despite repeated falls, we cheer every attempt, celebrating each step forward. However, when going after our own goals, we often resort to self-criticism at the slightest bump. We allow our negative thoughts to often stop us from going after our dreams.

Why (and when) did we transition from being supportive cheerleaders to harsh critics of ourselves?

Imagine yourself in the shoes of that resilient toddler. Picture your younger self or a cherished little one learning to walk and facing this new task with determination. What words of encouragement would you offer as they fall and get back up again? Write it in the space below:

____

____

____

____

Starting today, let's look at shifting our self-talk. Whenever negative thoughts arise as you pursue your goals, envision yourself as the cheerleader of that brave child. Extend the same kindness and support to yourself and use the words of encouragement you just wrote. Visualize that toddler accomplishing their goal of walking, and in your case, picture yourself celebrating your accomplished goal and use your inner dialogue as a source of empowerment. Celebrate every small step forward.

Here's a simple activity: For the next 30 days, keep a note on your phone and track your inner conversations daily. Award yourself points for uplifting self-talk and subtract points for negativity. At the end of each day, reflect on your score. Are you in the positive or the negative?

1	2	3	4	5	6	7
8	9	10	11	12	13	14
15	16	17	18	19	20	21
22	23	24	25	26	27	28
29	30					

Remember, awareness is the first step toward change. Commit to this practice until positivity becomes more of your default mode of thinking, or at the very least, when negative thoughts do arise, you can quickly correct yourself and turn your thoughts into more empowering ones. Each positive daily score brings you closer to your future positive self and will pave the way for greater well-being, confidence, and happiness in your life.

POSITIVE
MINDSET

CHAPTER 2

THE DAILY DRIVE

Joel Anthony

THE DAILY DRIVE
Joel Anthony

I was born and raised in Montreal, Quebec. My mom was a teacher and a principal, and she ran a tight ship. I was fortunate to have this early discipline. Even though she was strict, I had a fun childhood, running around and playing sports and games. As a child, some of my fondest memories were of the summers when we went down to Antigua to spend time with my grandmother.

When I was younger, I was really into football and track and field. I used to love watching the sprinters at the Olympics, and it inspired me to see how fast I could run. I'm not sure if genetically I was going to be fast or if pushing myself helped me, because I was really fast for my age group and for my size. I was also a very big football fan. Those two sports were by far my first loves.

I also enjoyed watching basketball and playing it with my friends. I was a huge Michael Jordan fan and loved watching Shaq and others in the NBA.

In the third grade, I started playing football in a peewee league, and continued with football through ninth grade. That all changed, though, when I moved to a new school that didn't have a football team. They did have a basketball program, so I switched my focus to basketball. It's funny how things work out. That summer I also went through a growth spurt, growing from 6 feet to 6 feet 6 inches. It was hard to find clothes that fit me, so my mom took me shopping and I ran into Dwayne Richens, who was a well-known basketball player in the area. He commented on my height, asked me some questions about basketball, and then he recommended I join a basketball program at YMCA.

A schoolmate and I started going to the Y to play, and that's where I started to meet others in the basketball community. It was fun and also gave me a chance to play with lots of players. It gave me a sense of community. This is where I realized how important these community programs are for youth. There weren't a lot of skill development programs growing up back then, which would have really helped me, as I was so new to basketball.

After graduating from high school, I played at Dawson College, where I had two great coaches, Trevor Williams, and Wayne Yearwood. They're our local legends—they played with the Canadian National team and professionally. Another memorable coach was Michael Smith. My second year at college, I tried out for the top team, but I didn't make it, so I continued to play on the second team. I was naturally athletic and although I was still raw as a player, I had good timing for blocking shots. I started to learn more about the game of basketball and developed as a player with better competition. It was one of my most fun times playing basketball.

At the end of the second year, the head coach for the top team, Olga Hyrack, came to me and said, "You're playing with us next year, right?" Of course, I said yes. I played for part of my third year, however, I wasn't eligible most of the year due to my academics. This also happened in my first year at Dawson College, and I felt like I needed a change. I had always been enamored with the United States and felt like there was something more for me in the U.S.

The summer after my third year at Dawson College, I ended up joining a summer basketball team where we would travel and play in tournaments in the U.S. With a week's notice, I also ended up taking my SATs and surprised everyone when I had a decent score of 1020 to be eligible to qualify. Playing on the traveling team increased my visibility to schools in the USA, and I received a few recruitment offers. I accepted the offer to Pensacola Junior College.

My first year in the States was a huge adjustment and, of course, I was homesick, but fortunately, I had another great coach named Paul Swanson. I still didn't take school seriously and that first year I ended up being ineligible again. Becoming ineligible at Pensacola was my biggest wake-up call. I'd put all my work of lifting weights, working out, and learning skills on the court, but I had to also fix the mess I'd created in the classroom.

My first year at Pensacola was really tough. About halfway through, I called my mom and said, "Maybe you should just get me a plane ticket and just get me out of here. This might not be my thing." And my mom said, "Look, you made this decision, just continue to focus." My mom had the attitude that everything would eventually work out. **You just have to have faith and trust in what you're doing.** There's balance in the world. That's stuck with me for so long and helped me so much.

This was a turning point for me. I wasn't going to be just another kid from Montreal who tried to go to the States and came back home because it didn't work out.

I think failure is relative to how you see it. In my case, I felt like that moment was the last of my failures. That's the closest I came to wanting to quit on a bad day. Because if my mom had bought me a ticket, I probably would have just gone home. I wasn't playing because I was ineligible, and I wasn't doing the right things in school, but she told me to make the changes needed and see it through.

My second year at Pensacola, I really started to focus on my education and continued to put in the work to develop as a basketball player. Any time my poor schooling habits started creeping back in, coach Swanson said, "Look, if you mess this up, I'll send you back to Montreal on a bus and I'll never speak to you again." I straightened up. I put all my efforts into my education and basketball.

I realized the switch was understanding that when I was in those low moments, we all have, when things are difficult, you don't have to keep going over the cliff. **Look for different ways to regroup, focus and get locked in on the task and do what you need to do to turn it around.** So, when my grades slipped, I just figured out what I needed to do and locked in on that to get my grades back up. We always have the option to just leave

and say, "It didn't work out." But I'm not going to be the one to quit. Not on the court, and not in school.

I had a great second season at Pensacola and I started to get offers from division one schools. When Lew Hill, the assistant coach from the University of Nevada Las Vegas, reached out to me to see if I had made a decision, I lit up, because UNLV is a basketball school.

Throughout high school, college and my athletic career, I've always had the mindset of wanting to get better and to help my team win games. I'm competitive, so I don't care what it takes or what I have to do. I just want to get better, and I want to win.

I thought I could get a lot better practicing against Lou Amundson, who was on the team at the time. Because he was similar in height and athleticism, but had more experience playing division one, I knew I could learn a lot from him, so I was sold on UNLV.

I played the first year and was so determined to turn my education around that in my first year at UNLV I actually made the Dean's List!

Going into my second year at UNLV, after a discussion with my coach, we made a decision that I would redshirt the next year so I could focus on my skill development. The coaching team thought if I focused on my development the next season, and finished my last year strong, I could prepare to go pro.

That was a tough decision, and I remember calling my mom to talk to her about it. My mom was always supportive, and she said, "Just make sure you graduate."

The summer before my last year at UNLV, I played with the Canadian National Team. It was a tough experience as we played in a few international games, and we lost badly, plus I wasn't even playing.

In my senior year at UNLV, I struggled a little at the beginning because I hadn't been playing games over the summer. I continued to work hard and ended up finishing the season strong and was named the 2006-07 Mountain West Conference Defensive Player of the Year.

After my senior year, I hired Mike Higgins as my agent, who was extremely honest, telling me he didn't know if he could even get me an NBA workout. I stayed in Vegas and ended up training at a facility called Impact, getting ready for the draft. Athletes come from all over the country to train there.

Because I was always focused on getting better every day, when opportunities would present themselves, I was ready. I only had two days' notice before my first NBA workout. My agent called me to let me know that someone had backed out and the spot was mine if I wanted it. So I went to Phoenix, and my workout impressed them enough that they asked me to come back. That led to offers for workouts from a lot of other teams. So, I went from not knowing if I would get a workout to having multiple workouts all over the country.

It was a fun experience.

One of my workouts was with the Miami Heat. I played well in the game they scouted, even though the Heat were originally looking at another player. I caught their attention, and that ended up giving me an opportunity with them.

After the draft, I signed a partially guaranteed contract, and went to Miami for summer league, and then training camp after that. There were two spots open, with six or seven players fighting for those spots.

I just put everything I had into my game and kept focused on getting better every day. Some things I did really well and some of my skills still needed a ton of work.

I remember the last day of camp and we were all back at the hotel. The season was beginning the next day, so I called my agent to see if he'd heard anything about who made the team. He hadn't heard anything about me personally, however, he did tell me he heard they'd cut two guys. One of the players they cut was my carpool buddy who was a player I thought for sure had made it. My agent and I figured no news is good news.

So, the next day, I drove over to the arena by myself. I got there early as usual and went into the locker room for the players who were trying out, which was basically in the bathroom. You have to earn the right to be in the official locker room. But when I went in, everything was cleared out. No one's stuff was there. I asked one of the players what was going on, and he said, "I guess you'll figure it out." So, I asked the equipment manager where my stuff is, and he said, "It's around here somewhere."

I looked around the official locker room and saw my name on a locker. My jaw dropped. Both of the guys were smiling, and I couldn't believe it. I went crazy and ran out of the room, trying to keep my composure. Then I called my agent, and he didn't answer, so I left a message with the news. And then called my mom, who is the busiest woman in the world, who also didn't answer. I left her a message, too. I told her, "We made it. This is the start for us."

At my first practice as a signed Miami Heat player, I had so much energy and adrenaline. It was like I was flying, grabbing every rebound because the adrenaline was pumping through me. I'm over here with Dwyane Wade, Shaq, Alonzo, Jason Williams, and Antoine Walker; all these players that I used to watch.

I will always remember, D Wade had come in, and he said, "Hey, welcome to the family."

I played in the NBA for 10 years. I was with the Miami Heat for seven years and won two NBA Championships in 2012 and 2013. Halfway through my seventh year, I was traded to the Boston Celtics. I also played with the Detroit Pistons and the San Antonio Spurs.

After the NBA, I went to Argentina and played two years in Buenos Aires with San Lorenzo. We won two South American League championships and two Argentinian league championships.

Throughout my career as athlete and now, as the General Manager of the Montreal Alliance in Canadian

Elite Basketball League (CEBL) I am especially grateful for the strong principles and guidance my mother provided. My mom is a very strong woman of faith, and she always taught me to trust in the Lord, and to believe that **if we keep doing the right things, even during tough times, and put in the work, we will reap the rewards in the long run!**

ABOUT JOEL ANTHONY

Joel Anthony is a former professional basketball player who has played in the National Basketball Association for ten years. He played for the Miami Heat, Boston Celtics, Detroit Pistons, and San Antonio Spurs. He won two championships with the Miami Heat in 2012 and 2013. Joel continued his professional career in Argentina, playing with San Lorenzo, where he won

two South American League championships and two Argentine league championships.

Currently, Joel is the General Manager of the Montreal Alliance of the Canadian Elite Basketball League (CEBL).

Check out this short video
for a message from Joel on
Persistence and Perseverance!

REFLECTIONS ON RESILIENCE

One thing that stood out in Joel's story is his focus on continuous growth and improvement at every stage of his athletic journey. He always wanted to contribute to his team's success, driven by his competitive spirit and his desire to excel. Even when he was just starting out in basketball, his focus was on genuine learning and progress. Joel's story serves as a powerful reminder that the path to success is paved with continuous learning, hard work, trusted mentors, and faith in the process.

What if we were to apply Joel's mindset in our own lives, committing to continuous improvement in our own endeavors? Whether it's in pursuing personal passions or excelling in our professional careers, there's tremendous value in committing to daily growth. Reflecting on your own life, are you actively challenging yourself to improve? Are there areas where you feel a sense of excitement and possibility, where you're eager to challenge yourself and expand your horizons? Think about one goal or activity that you've always wanted to pursue. Perhaps it's mastering a new language, acquiring a new skill, excelling in a sport, or advancing in your studies or professional career. Write one of your short-term goals in the space below.

Consider how you can dedicate yourself to incremental progress each day, with a mindset of continual growth.

In the space provided below, write down your commitment to embracing the journey of improvement in this particular area of your life by writing, "I focus on getting better every day."

___

Remember, the journey of personal growth is a continuous and rewarding process. By embracing the mindset of continual improvement and finding joy along the journey, you'll not only achieve your goals but also experience a deeper sense of fulfillment and purpose in your daily life.

55

CHAPTER 3

EMBRACING THE GRIND

Dr. John Frank

EMBRACING THE GRIND

Dr. John Frank

I was born and raised in Pittsburgh, Pennsylvania, with my three sisters. My dad was a lawyer and also a standout athlete in basketball and baseball. My mother was a homemaker, and we were a pretty traditional Jewish family. As a kid, I aspired to be a surgeon or an athlete. Sports always taught me important lessons, and I value those. My perspective on sports has shifted over time, but the resilience stories within them still resonate strongly with me.

Growing up, I played a lot of sports. Basketball was a big part of my life. We had a hoop in our backyard, and I had great skills. I won the city championship in one-on-one basketball around 10th grade. Then there was football, which is huge in Pittsburgh, and I played football from the time I could throw and catch. In high school, I played baseball for a while, and track was in the mix for a bit. But I focused on football; I was a powerhouse player and in high school, I had a great senior year.

One lesson that's stuck with me through my life came from Dan Radakovich, a legendary football coach who was connected to the Pittsburgh Steelers. He could be a little eccentric, the type of person I really cherish now. Somehow, my father was able to get me a session with him when I was in ninth or tenth grade. We met at the high school field on a Sunday afternoon. I had a bag full of balls and some kicking tees and blocking dummies. But we walked over to the goalpost, just the two of us. The coach said, "I want you to squat down and put your arms around the goalpost." I thought, well, this is strange, but OK.

"You got it?" he asked. I nodded, and he said, "Hug it tight like you mean it. Now, I want you to lift the goalpost out of the ground. Lift it."

Well, as you may know, the goalposts are anchored in cement. "You mean lift it out of the ground?" I asked.

"Yes, I just want to see your technique, how you go about lifting this. Lift this thing out of the ground!" he said. So, I squatted down and put my shoulder into it.

Impossible, right? But I tried. Veins were popping out of my head. Finally, he said, "OK, you can stop." As I relaxed, he continued, "You know that feeling you just had of exertion?"

"Yeah," I said. "I didn't move it."

"I want you to imprint that feeling you had for just five seconds," he said.

That was the lesson. He was done. It wasn't about actually lifting the post. **That struggle, that effort—he wanted me to channel that into every play of the game.** That lesson, about exerting yourself to the maximum, is something I've carried with me always and like to pass on to others.

After high school, I played for the Ohio State Buckeyes football team, where I was the starting tight end from 1980 to 1983. One thing I'm proud of is holding the record of catching more passes than any other tight end in Ohio State's history. As a senior, I was selected as a member of the university's Varsity Hall of Fame. In 1984, I was drafted by the San Francisco 49ers in the second round of the NFL draft and I played there for five seasons.

Used with permission of The Ohio State University

The 49ers made it to two Super Bowls during the time I played for the team. The Super Bowl was incredible, an event that's as much about fanfare and media and swag as it is the game. I was very lucky to be around amazing athletes, part of the winning team in 1985. Then I was able to play in a second Super Bowl. So, I played in my first year and my last, winning again right before I left the game to work on becoming a doctor—it felt like a full circle moment.

For me, football was a dream, but it wasn't my ultimate goal. My focus was always on medicine, and football was a means to that end. It was my priority from the beginning, and the sport was a way to get me there. I actually attended my first year of medical school while playing in the NFL. After achieving what I could in football, it was time to fulfill my primary dream of practicing medicine. Now I am a board-certified oto-laryngologist and a facial plastic surgeon specializing in hair restoration for scalps and eyebrows. I've worked in this specialized field for 25 years and have helped more than 20,000 patients.

Photo taken by: Al Golub (https://golubphoto.com)

Honestly, challenging days are more common than not. There are many days when it's tough, and you feel like you could quit. That's life, though, isn't it? If you're not feeling challenged, you're probably not pushing yourself enough. In my professional career, now as a doctor, I often ask myself why I stack my schedule so tightly with no breaks, but then I end up doing it again. It's about constantly pushing your limits. **It seems like**

when we're pushed to our limits, that's often where we grow the most. Even if you're great at your business, it seems there's always something more. There are days when I'm ready to give up all the time.

When I feel like giving up, all I have to do is remember that lesson from Coach Radakovich—about giving everything your all. For me, it's about striving for excellence, whether in my practice as a doctor or at home as a husband and father. It's different for everyone. You have to continually work on your relationships, your job, yourself—I draw inspiration from others, from seeing people overcome more significant challenges than mine.

Photo taken by: Al Golub (https://golubphoto.com)

The key is to prepare for the bad days on your good days. For me, meditation helps, as does being honest with yourself and others. The security and confidence you develop on good days can help you when times are tough. Confidence is also key. When I played on the 49ers, Coach Bill Walsh was an example of this. He exuded inner confidence, and you could see it. This is something I've remembered over the years. Being secure in who you are will take you a long way. So, invest in your good days to get through the bad ones. It's also about having a support system you can rely on, your inner circle, people who are there for you when you need it most.

I was a passionate football player and I'm a passionate surgeon. As much as I loved the game, I love helping people more!

ABOUT JOHN FRANK, M.D.

Dr. John Frank was a standout college football player at Ohio State who went on to play five seasons as a tight end for the San Francisco 49ers of the National Football League from 1984 to 1988. The 49ers won two Super Bowls during that time. Even though he attended medical school classes at Ohio State during the off-season, John returned to medical school full time. He is an otolaryngologist, board-certified by the American Board of Otolaryngology and the American Board of Hair Restoration Surgery. He became a Fellow of the American  College of Surgeons, an Assistant Professor of Clinical Otolaryngology at Columbia University College of Physicians and Surgeons and The Ohio State University College of Medicine-adjunct. He was inspired by one of his mentors to move from head and neck surgery to become a hair restoration surgeon.

Join John in embracing the beauty of sunny days while nurturing inner strength for the challenges ahead!

REFLECTIONS ON RESILIENCE

When was the last time you truly gave your all—your absolute best to an activity, a goal, or a dream? Picture that impactful moment when John shared an experience with the late Coach Dan Radakovich, a mentor John admired, where the coach challenged John to grasp a goalpost tightly and attempt to lift it from the ground. Picture it: a young athlete, veins popping, sweat pouring, gripping the goalpost as the coach urged him to give even more. John gave himself entirely, embodying the concept of giving his absolute best.

The focus wasn't on honing sport-specific skills; it went beyond, emphasizing the importance of exertion. This lesson became a guiding principle for John throughout his athletic and professional journey. Honored at Ohio State with titles such as two-time Academic All-American, Team MVP, inclusion in the All-Century Ohio State Football Team, and induction into Ohio State's Varsity Hall of Fame, John's dedication continued to the NFL. He earned two Super Bowl Championships (XIX, XXIII), contributing to one of the longest drives in NFL history by catching a crucial pass from Joe Montana during Super Bowl XXIII. This commitment also carried over into his professional life, where John, now a successful medical professional, owns thriving practices in Columbus, Ohio and New York City.

In soccer, we have a saying, "Go Hard for Five." When a player calls it on the field, it signals a collective effort from the team to focus and elevate their play for the next five minutes. It's about running faster, tackling harder—giving that extra push to boost energy on the field.

Go Hard for Five isn't restricted to a specific timeframe; it embodies the principle of doing more. Whether you have fitness goals or business aspirations, consider adding five minutes to your workout or making ten more sales calls in your day. It's about that additional effort, that push.

Where in your life will you Go Hard for Five? Share it in the space below:

____

If you have an accountability partner(s) or work on a team, consider sharing this principle with them, where everyone commits to Go Hard for Five on a monthly challenge or team goal. When you work together to push each other, the impact is magnified.

Embrace the powerful lesson Coach Radakovich taught John and, in your own life, commit to Go Hard for Five when pursuing your goals and dreams. Not only will you achieve them faster, but you'll also experience a profound sense of accomplishment, knowing you've given your very best!

GRIT

68

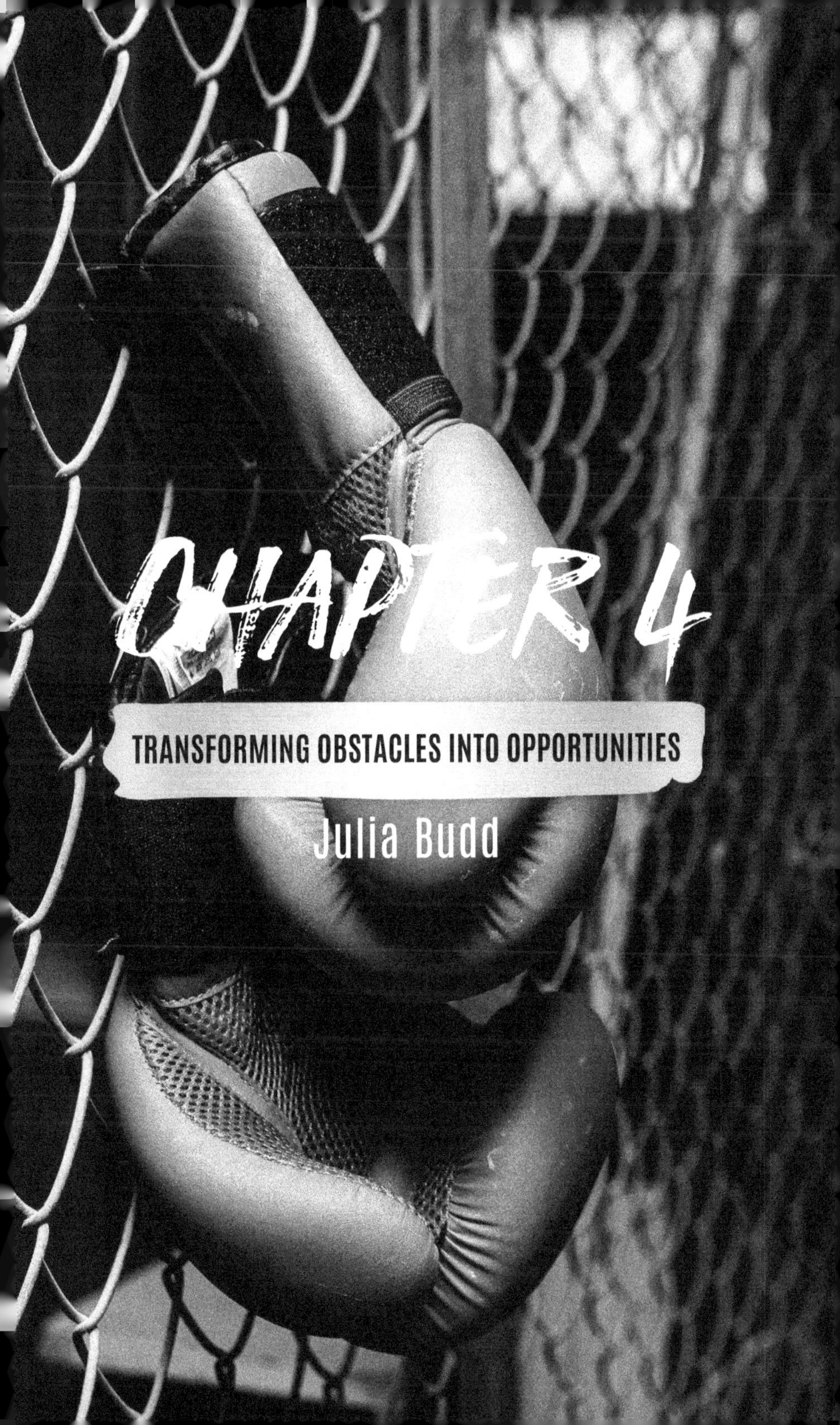

CHAPTER 4
TRANSFORMING OBSTACLES INTO OPPORTUNITIES
Julia Budd

TRANSFORMING OBSTACLES INTO OPPORTUNITIES

Julia Budd

I grew up in Roberts Creek on the Sunshine Coast, British Columbia, Canada. It is located on the southern mainland coast, across from Vancouver Island. My favorite childhood memories were playing in nature with my brother and sisters. All my friends were boys, and I would always try to keep up with them or compete with them in sports and outdoor games like Kick the Can. We were always running around, building forts, and climbing trees. Even though we were all friends, I was always competing—and I was persistent!

My dad and I also watched track and field in the Olympics, and I remember watching Jackie Joyner-Kersee win. She inspired me and I wanted to be just like her when I grew up, be known for my sport and reaching the medal podium. My dad and I also watched boxing. I vividly remember watching the famous "Super Fight" between Marvelous Marvin Hagler and Sugar Ray Robinson. The excitement in our home was electric, and I just wanted to be part of something that special one day.

One of my oldest childhood friends started Muay Thai at 15. She knew I would enjoy it, so I went with her for a trial and never looked back. And of course I loved it immediately. My first coach, Gabriel, saw the potential in me and helped me find my love for the sport.

Muay Thai is sometimes called "The Art of Eight Limbs," because it's primarily a striking-based martial art from Thailand and you fight in a ring. You use punches, kicks, elbows, and knee strikes—stand-up fighting styles. Muay Thai fighters have to use the full range of their bodies, and we focus on precision and power. The sport is known for its rigorous training, discipline, and respect for tradition.

On the other hand, MMA is really a hybrid combat sport that incorporates techniques from Muay Thai, Brazilian Jiu-Jitsu, wrestling, boxing, and Judo. And you fight in a cage. Here you'll see a lot of different fighting techniques because fighters are allowed to strike, grapple, and fight on the ground. When I moved into this, I had to train for diversity in my movements, and master new skills in ground fighting.

Mixed martial arts and Muay Thai kickboxing have come a long way since I started, as far as regulations, rules, and governing bodies. When I started, many of those rules and regulations were not in place. I remember my parents being terrified coming to see my fight in Tukwila,

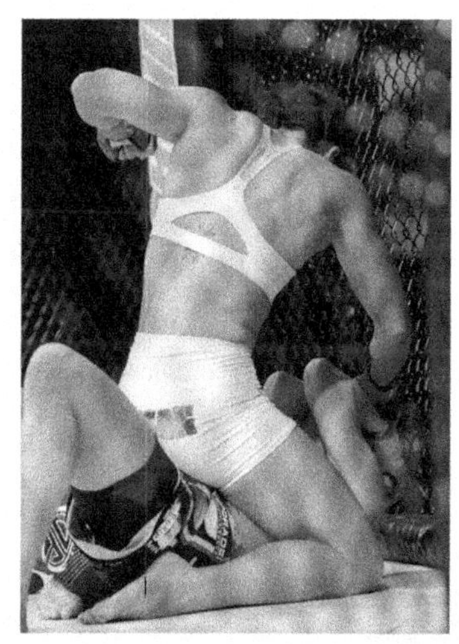

Photo taken by: G. Powers Photography (gpowersphotography.com)

Washington, at a little casino bar. There were about 150 people watching, and my parents were so nervous. They couldn't believe I was going to get into the ring! But after the fight, they realized how much I loved it and from then on they totally supported me endlessly.

Because it was so hard to get fights for me, I would sometimes go a year or longer in between competitions. I stayed motivated in training by setting goals for myself and always learning new things and perfecting what I was good at. I also loved researching strength and conditioning and went to school to learn about training programs and how to become a better athlete. Journaling was also a big part of my effort to stay disciplined and consistent. I journaled almost every day, rated my training level, and wrote down my goals for the next day.

I'm thankful to another one of my coaches, Lance Gibson Sr., and to Lance Gibson Jr., as they both never allowed me to stay down. When I transitioned to MMA, I was able to learn so much about wrestling and grappling from them. Lance Gibson Sr. would always tell the truth, even when it was difficult but necessary. I'm also grateful to my training partner Paul, who always came in with a positive attitude.

As a competitive athlete, it was important for me to remain committed to my training program, focusing on workouts, proper nutrition, and sleep. I also valued making time for friendships and fun. One funny memory that stands out for me is the day I had just finished working out, and my friend showed up at the gym and said there was an extra spot to go skydiving. An hour later, I was jumping out of a plane. These moments of spontaneity also added excitement to my life, so my life wasn't all strict discipline.

After transitioning to MMA, a fight was booked for me against Ronda Rousey in Strikeforce (a MMA and kickboxing organization). In the weeks leading up to the fight, my training schedule was intense, often consisting of six hours a day with up to three training sessions per day. The fight against Rousey was tough and challenging for me. My arm was dislocated, and I went home feeling incredibly discouraged and frustrated, focusing on what I couldn't do in my fight. It was my fourth MMA fight and the second fight that I had lost. Shortly after I got home, I received a letter telling me I'd been released by the Ultimate Fighting Championship (UFC), who had bought the Strikeforce organization. Well, that letter took me to a whole new low. I was feeling sorry for myself and hovered in that mindset for a good while.

I'm grateful to a friend of mine who helped me realize I needed to shift my mindset. Yes, my arm was in a sling, and I had just been released from the UFC, and my friend said, **"Well, what can you do?"** In that moment, I realized I could still work my lower body without my arms, and I could work on shifting my mindset. And then I got to work.

Within six weeks, I was back to doing pull-ups and training on the mats, working around my injury. **I realized no matter how bad something is, you can**

always find a way to do something. Eight months later, I was back in the cage and won my fight in the first round.

In retrospect, I am so grateful for that day because it shifted me to develop a different set of skills that I had been ignoring and began to work on my mental strength and attributes. Looking back on that first year in MMA, I hadn't really learned enough on the ground. I wasn't well-rounded enough. I was a great

Photo taken by: G. Powers Photography (gpowersphotography.com)

kickboxer, but my grappling and wrestling was my weakness. After that fight with Rousey, I dedicated the next year to learning more wrestling and grappling, and I would go on to being nine years undefeated. I credit that win streak to losing two important fights that first year that really helped me evolve my game. In 2017, I was crowned Bellator MMA featherweight champion and held that title until 2020. So, because I didn't quit, I am a four-time world champion.

My favorite quote has inspired me throughout my journey to becoming a champion in my sport is by Muhammad Ali: "The fight is won or lost far away from witnesses—behind the lines, in the gym, and out there on the road, long before I dance under those lights."

It's so true. **The hard work is done out of sight, and the drive to consistently show up and do the work is what will put you on top.** It's humbling to see the media and others say that I've made a profound impact on the sport, particularly within the featherweight division, and talk about "distinguished performances" and "significant victories." But it's also what I've worked for my entire life. So, I'm proud of my journey. I wanted to be a trailblazer in my chosen sport, and I feel like I've succeeded.

Photo taken by: G. Powers Photography (gpowersphotography.com)

And I haven't stopped. I'm still competing in MMA and boxing, and I volunteer, teaching wrestling and youth MMA and kickboxing on the Sunshine Coast and

Port Moody. I have a private gym on the Sunshine Coast at my home, and we also have an MMA gym in Port Moody. Teaching martial arts and training will always be a part of my life. **It's something I'm passionate about and love—it's an amazing feeling being able to inspire and help people reach their goals and dreams.**

ABOUT JULIA BUDD

Julia Budd is a kickboxer and mixed martial artist. A notable figure in women's combat sports, Julia transitioned from Muay Thai to Mixed Martial Arts (MMA) around 2010. Before moving to MMA, Julia had established herself as a formidable Muay Thai competitor, showcasing her striking skills in various matches. Her decision to switch

to MMA was driven by the desire for new challenges and the growing opportunities for female fighters in the sport.

Julia made her professional MMA debut in 2010, at Strikeforce Challengers 11 against Shana Olsen and secured a victory via technical knockout (TKO) in the second round. This fight marked the beginning of her career in MMA, where she went on to achieve significant success, including winning the Bellator Women's Featherweight Championship.

Her transition from Muay Thai to MMA allowed her to utilize her striking prowess while also developing a well-rounded skill set to compete effectively in the MMA world. Julia's journey from Muay Thai to becoming a champion in MMA is a testament to her dedication, adaptability, and skill as a martial artist.

Check out Julia's uplifting message on overcoming life's challenges!

REFLECTIONS ON RESILIENCE

Have you ever faced discouragement and heartbreak when falling short despite giving your all to achieve a goal? I'm sure we all have at some point. The sting is often intensified when, in addition to missing the mark, you may find yourself dealing with physical or additional emotional pain.

Maybe, like Julia, you've experienced an injury during competition or training. Alternatively, you might have missed out on a new job or a desired job promotion. Perhaps you received a lower grade than anticipated on a project or excelled in business without the corresponding acknowledgment or reward.

Take a moment in the space below to reflect on an experience from recent times that didn't unfold as planned.

____

____

____

Now, let's revisit that scenario. First, applaud yourself for putting forth your best effort. Next, imagine yourself in a similar situation again, and jot down five things you *CAN* do.

____

____

____

Throughout our lives, there will inevitably be moments where, despite our best efforts, we don't achieve our desired outcome. It's crucial to acknowledge and process the associated emotions before shifting our focus forward. Next, celebrate yourself for giving your best effort and keep in mind the empowering question, "What CAN I do?" Commit to yourself going forward that you will ask yourself this question when faced with unexpected setbacks and concentrate on the actionable steps within your control. Commit to yourself that you will be the person to ask your friends and family this powerful question when they also face their own setbacks and challenges.

I appreciate Julia's wise words: "No matter how bad something is, you can always find a way to do *something*."

Identify that something (or somethings), embrace it, and take action as you continue your journey toward realizing your goals and dreams!

RESILIENCE

82

CHAPTER 5

DIRECTING YOUR DESTINY

Ronnie Jagday

DIRECTING YOUR DESTINY

Ronnie Jagday

Growing up in Canada, I have many childhood memories of my dad telling me stories about how India had won eight Olympic Gold Medals in field hockey. He grew up playing field hockey in the streets of Ludhiana, Punjab, a field hockey hotbed, whereas for me, it was the typical sports that many Canadian kids played: soccer, basketball, tennis, baseball. In fact, it was practically every sport except field hockey! My dad had an ambition to be on the Indian National Team, and he made it to the combined Indian Universities team (the equivalent of the Indian Junior National Team, one may say).

My grandfather was a very strict civil engineer who kept telling my dad to focus on his education and not field hockey. My dad was passionate about the sport and instead of focusing on his education, he decided to come to Canada in the 70s to pursue his dream of coaching. He boldly went to the office of the President of Canada's national field hockey team and asked for a job. After some banter and more than a little disrespect, which my father put aside, four years later my father was the coach of both the Men's Junior and Senior National teams.

I remember as a young child going to Vancouver International Airport and greeting the National team after they won the Pan American Championships Gold Medal. There were hundreds of people waving Canadian flags as they arrived, celebrating the fact the National Team qualified for the 1984 Olympics to be held in Los Angeles. It certainly made a lasting impression on me, and I remember dreaming that one day, I too would compete in the Olympics. So, sports have been a really big part of my life, always.

In spite of being surrounded by field hockey, I didn't play the sport. I continued to focus on other sports, enjoying the variety and competition. People were always asking me when I would take up field hockey, but I never felt pressured by my dad. Where I really found success was in tennis, and I won a second-place ranking in British Columbia for under-14s. I was excited about this as a potential avenue for scholarships and achievement.

One thing about playing a lot of different sports is, along the way, you learn a lot of skills that cross over into other sports. Everything I learned from playing basketball, tennis, and soccer was quite transferable. And it's not like I never played field hockey. I would play in the house or out and about with my dad. Eventually, I started playing in a field hockey league. I picked up on it quickly and started scoring goals. Our club team went to Los Angeles for a Cal Cup Tournament, one of the biggest hockey tournaments in the world. Next, I tried out for and made the Provincial B.C. team, and following that, the junior national team. I did have a full training schedule with the junior national team and still up until grades 11 and 12, I continued to play soccer, tennis and basketball. Eventually, as you get older, the more you start to specialize, and I started funneling until, at age 18, I was focused purely on field hockey.

Once I settled here, my dedication led me to join the junior national team, part of the "Project 2000" initiative aimed at nurturing future Olympians. My journey with the team was a blend of training, competition, and personal growth, and I ended up going with the team to the 2000 Olympics at the age of 23.

While these achievements were all amazing, the pay for professional field hockey is not that of other professional sports, like basketball or soccer. One of the guys from the U.S. field hockey team called me and suggested I come to Silicon Valley to interview for Cisco (a digital communications technology company). I'd been dabbling in the stock market a little bit, so I was intrigued, figuring, what do I have to lose flying down for an interview?

Instead of asking about my work experience, they spent a lot of time talking about sport and the Olympics and how that translates to corporate life, and they offered me the job. I had to fly home to wait for my visa, and in that short time, Cisco announced the market had turned and it was laying off 7,500 people. At this point, I'd accepted their offer for a salary and moving expenses but had told them I am still on the national team and not sure I want to give that up at just 23. They agreed it would be good for the

Photo credit: Omari Aldridge

company for me to keep playing. And in the end, I didn't get laid off.

The lessons learned from sports, such as discipline, teamwork, and goal-setting, were valuable in my new role at Cisco. I was basically a "water boy" to the stars, managing logistics and purchasing and keeping things running smoothly. During this time, I was also flying back to Vancouver every weekend to practice with the field hockey team, so I was really burning it at both ends.

My experience at Cisco, though, also opened the door to entrepreneurship, and led me and my mentor to start a successful tech business, buying and reselling components for high-tech companies like Cisco and Facebook. With the money I was making, I started investing into real estate. I eventually retired from field hockey in 2008 to focus on my entrepreneurial and personal life. And to be honest, I was a little burned out. There's a lot of politics and unseen competition in sports, and I fought that battle for long enough.

My goal had always been to make it back home to Vancouver. In 2019, after a successful exit of our business, I was able to return home to my native Vancouver.

Today, as I look back on going from amateur team sports to the Olympics and then from a business owner to a real estate entrepreneur, the core values learned through my athletic career remain central. When things aren't going the way I like in my life, I remember the lesson one of my sports psychologists, Dr. Saull Miller, shared. **He told me our minds are like a TV set and we control the channel. If you are receiving inputs you don't like, then change the channel. Change your mindset.**

I also like to remind myself, **"You are the average of the people around you"**. I learned this from a young age, to be around people who influence for good, and I've thought that way all my life. It has equipped me to be ready for a fight, to be confident, and know what I can accomplish.

Photo credit: COA/COC

Looking back on my journey as an athlete, I learned early on that adversity is part of the path to greatness. I've found it challenging to pinpoint a single "bad day." Many of my most difficult days came as a result of injuries. Throughout my athletic career, I remember those agonizing days spent confined to a bed, dealing with pain from ankle injuries, hamstring strains, or quad pulls.

I've had many injuries over my career, and every time I was discouraged and restricted from training and competing due to injury, I would hold on to the belief in myself and the notion that my goal is worth pushing through the difficult days. Focusing on my ultimate goal helped me persevere.

I realize that those difficult times were not just tests of my physical strength, but of my mental strength as well. Bouncing back from injury made me realize how badly I really wanted to achieve my goals.

The resilience I learned through sport helped me navigate through the challenges I experienced in my corporate and entrepreneurial endeavors. The transition from sports to business was seamless, thanks to the discipline and perseverance honed on the field.

ABOUT RONNIE JAGDAY

Ronnie Jagday is a former international field hockey player for the Canadian Men's National team, beginning his international career in 1998 against Spain. He contributed to Canada's gold medal win at the 1999 Pan American Games and competed in the 2000 Summer Olympics.

Ronnie transitioned to a business career in 2001, where he continued to play field hockey, training on weekends, through 2008. During this time, he also earned a B.S. in Business Administration from San Jose State University and completed advanced studies in Project & Program Management at Stanford University, earning a Certified Project Manager Credential. He also founded and eventually sold a tech company before moving back to Vancouver.

With over 15 years of experience, Ronnie has led high-performance teams and managed multi-million-dollar projects globally. His leadership is characterized by a commitment to positivity, continuous learning, and uplifting others.

Tune in to hear Ronnie's inspiring words of encouragement!

REFLECTIONS ON RESILIENCE

Ronnie has achieved remarkable success in his professional and investment endeavors, drawing upon principles learned from his athletic career, with a powerful mindset being a crucial component.

A gem shared by Ronnie likens the results we see in our life to a show we are watching on TV. I encourage you to consider this: If the results in your life are not what you want or like, change the channel. Make the decision to do something different; after all, switching channels is as simple as deciding.

The term "decision" has Latin roots in "decide," originating from "decidere," meaning OFF + CUT. Each decision involves cutting something off; in this context, reducing negative influences and infusing positive inputs will create transformative outputs. Commit to daily growth and learning, a step that deserves kudos as you read this book.

Some examples of intentional growth may involve reading, listening to inspiring podcasts, watching uplifting YouTube videos, and attending personal development and leadership events.

In the space below, write down one of your short-term goals. It may be one you have already written down in a previous Reflections on Resilience section, or it may be another short-term goal.

____

____

____

____

Next, think of one positive input you can add to help you accomplish your goal and dream.

For instance, if your goal is a promotion at work or to take your business to the next level, find a podcast, YouTube, or book that focuses on a relevant skill set. If you have fitness goals or are an athlete looking to excel to the next level, join a gym, hire a coach or learn about new skills, incorporating an extra 15 to 30 minutes of daily training.

Make a decision today to add a new positive input. Write it in present tense to declare your decision.

For example:

I listen to one educational podcast every day.

Your turn:

____

____

____

____

Remember, you can choose your inputs, and your success will be the result of your intentional decisions. If the current show isn't captivating, change the channel. Keep intentionally growing, and keep making those positive decisions to move you forward. Your goals and dreams are waiting for you!

94

DISCIPLINE

CHAPTER 6

RISING TO GREATNESS

Scott Morgan

RISING TO GREATNESS

Scott Morgan

I was super energetic as a child, always outside, riding bikes, exploring the great outdoors. Even as a toddler, I caused my parents a fair amount of worry with my daredevil stunts. Before I even turned two, I was jumping up and down poles on playgrounds, climbing rope ladders, scaling the refrigerator, and leaping off the kitchen counter—I was a very adventurous kid.

My fearlessness both amused and alarmed my family, so my parents enrolled me in gymnastics when I was four. Even though they meant it to be an outlet for my energy, within 6 months, I was quickly moved into the competitive program. I wasn't quite ready and made a mockery of my first competition. So, the minimum age for gym-

nastics competitions in B.C. is now five, so kids are a little more disciplined.

Growing up, we lived right beside a forest with a lot of trails, so I spent a lot of time on my bike and running with my friends. I was lucky to have parents who gave me many opportunities and supported me in playing a lot of different sports and activities. Even though some of my coaches discouraged it, I believe the variety of sports really fueled my competitive spirit.

In gymnastics, you start by learning all events. I did Men's Artistic Gymnastics, which is the six events you see in the Olympic games: floor exercise, pommel horse, still rings, vault, parallel bars, and horizontal bar. Most kids do all six until their late teens, then specialize in select events if it benefits their team.

For me, sports have always been social, even though all the sports I've done have been individual sports. When I was 12, the entire group I was training with quit gymnastics. The next group available to train with was the 8-year-old group—quite a big age gap. This was really tough for me, so I actually ended up leaving competitive gymnastics, thinking I'd never go back to it. I love the sentiment around the theme of this book, "never quit on a bad day," because I feel like I got the opportunity to quit on a good day. Before I left the competitive program, I would often find myself on the way to the gym, telling my parents in the car that I wanted to go home and just wasn't feeling it. Although they never explicitly said "never quit on a bad day," they would respond with understanding, acknowledging that I wasn't feeling up to it, and suggesting that we could revisit the conversation another day. They didn't want to force me into anything or allow me to make a decision I might later regret by leaving gymnastics on a "bad day." I could tell how tough it was for them because they saw my potential and my coach saw my potential, but it didn't matter if I wasn't happy, and my heart wasn't in it. On a good day, we made the decision to leave competitive gymnastics. I am grateful for what my parents were able to do for me in helping me make that decision.

At this point, I had also just started high school, and I was really excited to meet new people and try new sports. Though I was no longer competing for my gym club, I still flipped around informally in gymnastics throughout high school.

After a few years of participating in my high school gymnastics team, I had become close peers with a few other gymnasts from other schools, most notably my buddy Will from a neighboring high school. In my last year of high school, a former Swiss Junior National Team gymnast attended Will's school on an exchange and Will convinced him to join their high school gymnastics team. Naturally, we all became really close friends. Having more competition kind of fueled that competitive fire because I had someone locally who was better than me and it inspired me to train harder.

Having met more peers in gymnastics, I really started to enjoy gymnastics again - it rekindled my passion for the sport. After I graduated, Will had goals of competing on the Provincial (British Columbia) gymnastics team and, with a little persuasion, convinced me to go back to regular competitive gymnastics training. Together, we paid a visit to my old gym club, Flicka Gymnastics, to see if they would let us come back and train again.

Coach Toma, the head coach of Flicka, who moved me into the competitive program when I was 4 years old, let us come back and train in the drop-in times. After a few weeks, we wanted more, so he agreed to supervise us for an extra day during the week. Will and I wanted to do competitions, so we started researching and watching videos to learn what skills we needed to perform to compete. I learned over 20 new skills in two months. Coach Toma realized we needed more instruction and would benefit from being in a proper class, so he insisted to Coach Vali, my former coach, to let us in his group. But we were met with skepticism and a pretty blunt assessment: He'd give us two months, he said, because he felt our time had passed. I still remember him telling us in front of the others in our group, "Your ship has sailed. Your train has passed. You will never be a gymnast again." But Will and I were determined to prove otherwise. Will and I ended up being role models to the younger gymnasts in our group. **Whether we were sore, tired, or sick, we always showed up and worked hard to learn new skills.** It changed the dynamic in Coach Vali's group by motivating the younger gymnasts, and he loved that. We worked at pushing our limits.

Will's comeback took a severe turn when a training accident left him with a broken neck. Even though the doctors told him he'd be lucky to walk and wouldn't ever do gymnastics or stunts again, he was back in the gym seven months later. It motivated me to pursue gymnastics even harder. I had challenges of my own, including a near-fatal car accident, but we were so lucky to basically walk away from it. A few months later, I competed in my first competition. Soon after that, I qualified for my first nationals.

Along the way, the hard days built my confidence—and my resolve. I always had the support of my friends, family, and my coach. Coach Vali fought for me and was a key reason I had the opportunities I did, and eventually I made it to the national team.

We trained five days a week. When we started, I was working a heavy labor job full-time, so I would work and then drive straight to the gym, where we would typically train for four or five hours. So, I often took a nap when I got there.

I remember a moment when it all changed for me. During the 2010 Winter Olympics held in Vancouver, I was at a mall, and I noticed two athletes wearing their full national team kit walking in the mall. It instantly gave me shivers. A thought crossed my mind: imagine being halfway across the world, representing your country, wearing your country's colors.

So, that was the moment when I knew I wanted to compete for my country. That basically opened up an important conversation I had with my coach. I told him I wanted to compete at the senior elite level and represent Canada. I asked him what I needed to do, and he said, Nationals are in two months. You need to hit these scores on these events, or win your current level, to convince me that you're good enough. If you don't, then you need to spend another year in the Provincial stream before you move into the senior category.

So, I left my full-time job, uninsured my car, went back to working part-time to keep the bills paid and focused purely on gymnastics. After two months of focused training, and with my family watching, I won the all-around title in my level, along with three events at nationals: floor, rings, and vault. After this, Coach Vali and I hit the drawing board to build a plan for competing in the Senior category the following season.

Shortly into my Senior career, my strengths caught the eye of our National Team coach, who told me to stop all-around and focus on the 3 events I was best at. After a successful year of National qualifiers, I was added to a small team that went to Puerto Rico for a week-long training camp and competition. This was my first international competition, and I made the most of it, walking away with a bronze medal on vault. I didn't realize it at the time, but that was the start of qualifiers for my first PanAm games. I was also selected to potentially compete on the world championship team, the last before the 2012 Olympics. Talk about pressure to qualify!

After a challenging 2012 Olympic cycle for our men's gymnastics team, our national team revamped its coaching staff and strategy, giving me a chance to compete with our top team. In 2013, I competed at my first world championships. Dealing with a sinus infection, probably stemming from my pent-up stress heading into the competition, I qualified for Floor finals, the first time Canada had qualified for an event final in over 6 years.

So, as you can see, I had many different types of challenging days. Some are mentally challenging, in terms of someone doubting my abilities or having to face my fears. Sometimes you're just depleted. And sometimes you're facing an injury that could end your sports career. You never know if you're going to show up on a good or bad day, if you'll be sick or sore, if something personal happens and you have to show up and compete. You have no idea. So, you have to show up with a "no excuses" mentality and get through the difficult times. It really helped having a coach who understood the pressures that came from this, and who allowed me to vent and lean on him.

What I also learned was that when I pushed through the hard days, I actually built more confidence in myself. Having Will from the early days as my good friend, motivator and supporter was huge. We don't like to brag or hear others talk about our accomplishments, but he's so proud of me, and vice versa. It's really important to have this type of friend. There are times where you have to take a certain path, and for me, I had an awesome friendship circle and family that understood the sacrifices I needed to make to accomplish my goals.

One of my favorite quotes is, 'Everything you want is on the other side of fear.' I love the quote because it speaks so much to my experience and emotions when pursuing my goals. Throughout my athletic career, I've encountered numerous fears and even faced doubts from others. However, I've learned to persevere by keeping my dreams in focus and leaning on the encouragement of supportive friends and family. Because I pushed through my fears, I've been able to experience incredible highs and athletic success. **I encourage you to go after your goals with everything you have, even when the odds may seem stacked against you, because**

the journey toward your dreams is as rewarding as the destination!

ABOUT SCOTT MORGAN

Scott Morgan is an elite Canadian artistic gymnast who represented Canada at the 2016 Rio Olympics and was a multi-medalist at the Commonwealth Games. Starting gymnastics at age 4, he stopped competing in gymnastics in high school before returning in 2007 to train with a good friend. By 2011, he was competing internationally, including at two Pan American Games.

In 2014, Morgan was Canada's second-most decorated athlete at the Commonwealth Games with four medals. His career highlight came at the 2013 World Championships, where he was the first Canadian man since 2006 to qualify for an apparatus final. In 2018, he secured multiple medals at the Canadian Championships, Commonwealth Games, and the University of Calgary International Cup, excelling in the floor, rings, and vault events.

Scott is considered one of the best male gymnasts in Canada.

Watch this video to hear Scott's helpful tip on how finding what makes you tick will guide you to success!

REFLECTIONS ON RESILIENCE

Ever felt that ache? The one that lingers when someone throws doubt on your dreams and goals. Whether subtly conveyed or, like one of Scott's coaches, bluntly spoken, the impact is deep—a realization that someone questions your capabilities. Hearing words of disbelief is never easy.

Sometimes, this lack of belief comes from those closest to us, making it even more heartbreaking. Whether they are sharing their thoughts out of a desire to protect us or projecting their own limiting beliefs, the hurt remains the same.

Scott's coach candidly shared his doubts on what Scott and Will would be able to do, given their ages and time away from the sport. In later years, he acknowledged seeing a spark in Scott, believing that his words would fuel him. In Scott's case, they did.

In life, choices continually present themselves. Scott could have internalized his coach's doubts, letting them deflate him. Instead, he chose to harness those words as fuel, driving himself forward. This reminds me of a quote by Les Brown: "Someone's opinion of you does not have to become your reality." Scott focused on his dreams and goals, embracing and choosing the encouragement and belief from both his training partner Will and his family, and this even changed his coach's confidence in him.

Think about your own "Will"—someone who, when you shared a goal or dream, responded not with skepticism but with excitement and belief. This could be a friend, family member, training partner, teammate, colleague, mentor, teacher, coach, spouse, or pastor. Who has encouraged you along your journey, inspiring you not only with words but also with their own actions?

Take a moment to express gratitude to your "Will" in the space below:

____

____

____

____

____

Next, reach out to this person with a phone call, voice message, or video message, sharing the heartfelt message you've just written. Sending it in this manner allows them to hear your voice and truly feel the impact of their actions on your journey. Not only will they feel great, but you'll also feel inspired even more, too.

If you're fortunate to have more than one "Will" in your life, continue the practice by sending one voice or video message per day.

The people we choose to have around us play a pivotal role in either propelling us forward toward our dreams and goals or anchoring us in place. It's often said that we are the average of the five people we spend the most time with. So, who fills your time? Take a moment now to reflect on the individuals you choose to surround yourself with. If you're uncertain whether they act as a propeller or anchor in your life, consider how you feel after spending time with them.

If identifying your "Will" proves challenging, or the people you are spending the most time with are not inspiring you to move closer to your dreams and goals, that's okay. In this next season of life, intentionally become someone else's "Will," and you'll naturally attract a supportive presence to your own life. Seek out those who share similar interests or values — join hobby groups, clubs, attend networking events, find a church or small group, or volunteer in your community.

Choosing to be surrounded by positive influences is like having a reliable team by your side. They uplift you during challenges, celebrate successes, and contribute to an encouraging atmosphere that fuels personal growth. Being a part of a supportive community and focusing on their affirming messages are key factors in navigating life's journey with resilience and fulfillment.

BELIEF

CHAPTER 7

SCORING BIG BY SAYING YES

Jason Holder

SCORING BIG BY SAYING YES

Jason Holder

I grew up in Rowans Park, Saint George, Barbados, and from a very young age, playing cricket was my primary afternoon activity. I spent countless hours playing. Though I really loved cricket, my friends and I also played basketball and road tennis—any game was a welcome diversion. I did harbor a love for basketball, inspired by my uncles, yet it was cricket that really resonated with me.

It wasn't long before my aptitude for the game was recognized. My father, who never donned a sports jersey, decided to enroll me in a summer camp at Empire Sports Club when I was just 8 years old. Although that initial experience didn't develop as expected, my mother found another connection that led me to Wanderers Cricket Club, which became a second home. Playing regularly, I experienced my first international tour to England, at the age of 10—and it was this trip that really cemented my desire to make the sport of cricket my life.

Making it to the Barbados Under 13 cricket team was amazing. One thing that stands out for me during that time was scoring my first "100" in a U-13 game against Christchurch High School. A 100 is when a batsman scores 100 runs in an inning. It is a really big milestone that both fans and players celebrate (sometimes it's called a "century"). It's quite a remarkable accomplishment, and it was definitely a memorable highlight for me at a young age.

One of the most influential people in my early journey was Ezra Moseley, who I met at St. Michael's School when I was about 13 years old. He was instrumental in everything I achieved. He taught me the game, and the importance of discipline. He was a genius with the ball, and he taught me everything I know about bowling.

He was a hard task man, always focused on instilling the right principles in us. One memorable experience I have of him was when he was trying to teach us some manners (of course we didn't realize it at the time). He was our new coach, so I was excited to show him what I had. He told me to pad up, so I rushed in and in cricket, you take guard before you bat. So, I shouted "middle!" And coach said, "Hello." I thought he didn't hear me, so again I said, "Middle!" He said, "Excuse me." I thought, *what in the world is wrong with this guy's hearing? What does he want?* So, I shouted again as loudly as I could, "Middle!". Then he replied with a firm and serious voice, "Look, by the time I finish, you will all learn some manners. It's middle, please."

To this day, when I'm going to bat and you hear me ask for guard, you will also hear me say, "Middle please." He also taught us to be proud of our appearance, to tuck our shirts in and look the part. He taught us that people should know who we are, through our appearance, before we even opened our mouths to speak and interact with them. He helped me learn simple things like being kind, disciplined, humble, and confident, and valuing the simple courtesies.

This was really just the beginning, as I continued to excel. At age 11, I started playing on the Under 13 team, then at age 13, I moved on to the Under 15 team and next on to Under 17 and then Under 19. My path seemed to chart itself, leading me straight to the High Performance Academy after competing in the Youth World Cup in New Zealand.

I remember a challenging time for me was when I felt like I was in a lull in my career. My youth career was an extremely smooth path, and I figured it would be the same finishing Under 19 cricket and joining the High Performance Academy that I would walk right into the West Indies Cricket Team (this team represents several countries and territories in the Caribbean region) however it didn't happen that way. This actually led me to one of my biggest eye-opening experiences. Being part of the high performance academy was the first time I was ever exposed to a sports psychologist. I really knew nothing about what a sports psychologist does, what it entails. We had to go to mandatory scheduled team and individual sessions, but that's really all I would go to. I really thought to myself, *I don't need anyone telling me what to do. I'm fine. I'm perfect.* Initially, I thought it was a waste of time. However, after finishing at the High Performance Academy, at this time in my career, I was feeling a bit worried. The academy was based in Barbados, so I had access to the academy even though I was finished. I was really concerned and knew I needed to do something different. **I thought to myself, what's the worst thing that can happen** if I go see the sports psychologist. So, I said yes to the opportunity and took it seriously by attending one-on-one sessions with him. During this period, I learned a lot from see-

Photo credit: Action Plus Sports Images / Alamy Stock Photo

ing the psychologist, and the one-on-one work was one of the best things that's happened in my life. He helped me understand myself more than I ever had—how I am under pressure, when I'm tense, and even when I'm happy. He taught me about triggers and how to control my emotions when life seemed to be moving extremely fast. That's really important knowledge for athletes.

I did end up making the West Indies Men's Cricket Team (nicknamed the Windies) at a young age. They say talent opens doors, but for me, what helped was a lot of hard work and an insatiable love for the game.

Photo credit: PA Images / Alamy Stock Photo

Throughout my career, as a professional athlete, I've had many challenging days over the years, but never one that made me want to quit my sport. One of the most challenging, though, was when I was captain of the Windies Team, and it was the day I achieved my first five-wicket haul against India in Antigua. It was my first five-wicket haul and also a match-winning five-wicket haul. A five-wicket haul is when a bowler takes five or more wickets in a single inning. I've never really been one to show my emotion, but after that game, which we won, I remember coming into the dressing room and no one said anything. I went into the shower and started to cry. I just felt all the emotion because leading up to that it had been a really tough period for the team, and my captaincy had been called into question some. I'm a big team man, so that was tough for me. Previously, we were getting hammered in the series - we were struggling, and we needed something to not only lift us, but lift the people of the Caribbean as well, too. It felt great to perform under pressure and the way in which we won was exceptional. Even though it was a tough time, I pushed through because I don't like leaving something unfinished. I don't want to quit.

The captaincy itself was a big learning experience for me. I learned that leading is not just about strategic calls on the field; it's also about balancing politics, expectations, and managing a diverse team's morale. It was a role that matured me quickly, shaped my resolve, and taught me to navigate the pressure of an intense professional sport. We had plenty of struggles and harsh criticism, but giving up was never an option. My tenure as captain taught me

Photo credit: Anthony Devlin Photography / Alamy Stock Photo

resilience and the importance of honoring the process over the outcome.

Body language is a massive thing for me. I think it stems from the lessons I learned from Coach Moseley. I can tell a lot about somebody's character by the way they carry themselves. I have an energetic personality and I like to bring the vibes, especially as a captain. I know the only way I can transfer that infectious confidence throughout the dressing room is if I show it first. I want to make sure everybody is comfortable and confident because that's the only way we can get positive results. I like to carry myself in a way where people can tell that I'm vibrant, positive, and influential. **I believe we are also a product of our environment, so choose carefully who you put yourself around.** These are a few small yet important lessons I have learned over the years.

Photo credit: PA Images / Alamy Stock Photo

As an athlete participating in international sports, every day can be a tough one, but what makes those demanding days more manageable are the truly memorable experiences. To me, there's nothing sweeter than those moments while performing at the highest level. One particular day stands out like a dream come true—the day I secured my most significant Indian Premier League (IPL) contract. Through persevering on the toughest days, cricket has provided financial transformations and also life-changing experiences. Most importantly, it has played a pivotal role in shaping the person I am today. I also enjoy playing golf, so I'll liken it to golf. In golf, you hit a number of bad shots, but once you strike that one exceptional shot, it energizes you to push forward.

Through it all, my mantra has remained simple: keep smiling and be thankful. Life has a lot of unexpected turns, and you never know what will be coming at you next, so cherish what you have.

My journey might seem smooth when you look back at it this way, but I had the same trials any aspiring athlete and person goes through. For me, the difference came from valuing the process, embracing the tough days and even welcoming the grind. The wins, personal and for the team, have made every challenge worth facing.

ABOUT JASON HOLDER

Jason Holder is a Barbadian cricketer. He is a right arm medium-fast bowling all-rounder who features in all three cricketing formats: Test matches, One-Day Internationals and Twenty20 Internationals. In January 2019, Jason was ranked as the number one all-rounder in the world according to the official International Cricket Council Test rankings. Jason won the prestigious Lord Gavron Award in 2009, which is given to a Barbados under-19 cricketer who's been outstanding on the playing field.

Tune in as Jason breaks down the importance of sticking to simple processes to help you reach your dreams!

REFLECTIONS ON RESILIENCE

In the midst of a lull, Jason found himself worried and uncertain about the future of his athletic career. It was in this vulnerable state that he was open to doing something a little different, and he asked himself a simple yet profound question when deciding whether he should book individual sessions with a sports psychologist. He asked himself, "What's the worst that can happen?" This moment of introspection led him to embrace something new. This decision proved pivotal, as Jason learned incredible insights about himself that positively helped his athletic career and also left a lasting impact on his personal life.

One of my favorite quotes, "Life begins at the end of your comfort zone," by Neale Donald Walsch, reminds me of Jason's experience.

How often do we shy away from opportunities without realizing their potential to steer us toward our goals? Jason's courage in saying yes to the unknown shows us that some of the most rewarding and transformative experiences stem from initially intimidating situations.

Now, your turn. Have you ever found yourself in a situation where you were so worried about the outcome that you avoided it completely? Maybe it's a conversation you need to have, making a career move, starting a business, or beginning a new hobby or activity. Take a moment and ask yourself, "What's the worst that can happen?" Or, reflect on a time when you took action despite the fear, resulting in a positive outcome. Alternatively, share an experience where things didn't go as planned, or you grew as a person and learned valuable lessons for future tough situations. Share your thoughts below.

Remember to ask yourself the question, "What's the worst that can happen?" especially when encountering new experiences or unforeseen challenges. It might just be the key to unlocking new opportunities or navigating frustrations with resilience!

PASSION

124

CHAPTER 8

FINDING TRUE NORTH IN CHALLENGE

Andrea Neil

FINDING TRUE NORTH IN CHALLENGE

Andrea Neil

Bad days are such a funny concept. I've always believed that what constitutes a "bad" day depends so much on our state of mind. I think I learned that from my parents at a very early age. One of my best memories growing up was the pure joy of being outside and having lots of unstructured play. That's pretty amazing if you know that I was born with a dislocated left hip and that the doctors had told my parents that I'd never run well. But instead of restrictions, my parents gave me the freedom to fall and learn to get back up. This not only taught me resilience, but it was also the best kind of medicine and laid the foundation for my career.

If my parents had been worried about bad days, I think my life could have turned out very differently. They never showed any worry about my condition. Some of my best memories are being outside playing catch with my dad. My parents never let what the doctors said stop me from being outside and constantly on the move. I played all the time. Whether just around the neighborhood or on organized teams, I played every sport I could. Oftentimes, I had to play on the boys' teams because there was no other place for me to play. That wasn't uncommon back then. I loved the social aspect of it, too. Sports taught me cooperation, reciprocity, and coordination. I think when I was young, the drive for excellence was less about competition and more about bringing the best version of myself to the team. That became an ethic for me later on.

It wasn't easy, but I think those physical challenges are what taught me to work harder. When I was in pre-school, we also discovered I was going blind in my left eye. I just got on with it, playing with an eye patch and, at times, a compromised leg. But my focus was always on putting in 100 percent. I think there's a cute photo somewhere of a future Hall of Fame athlete in the soccer goal as a goalkeeper with a bad hip, an eye patch, and a hockey helmet on for protection.

I don't remember feeling competitive as a young child, but it certainly developed as I immersed myself in sports. I was seven when I started playing badminton, which ended up being my main sport until my teenage years. It's a quick game, and there's no cutting corners. I had dreams of playing internationally and made it to the junior national level. Soccer was different. Until Grade 12, I had only played in a recreational environment. When I was 17, I was invited onto a competitive Under 18 team and experienced the more high-performance type of environment I had been used to in badminton. I loved it.

Both badminton and soccer demanded their own training programs, but it was the crossover of skills from one sport to the other that helped shape me. In high school, I also played basketball, and learning how to do a layup taught me the technique of jumping off one leg in order to head a ball in soccer. That's a movement I never learned directly from soccer training.

Around the same time that I was really getting into competitive soccer, I was also approaching the age limit of the youth badminton category in Canada, which is Under 19. As a junior nation-

al-level player, I had some decisions to make. It's a whole different game when you transition from U-19. You're not the oldest anymore; you're the youngest now, and you're competing as an adult. The national team coach told me, "If you want to take your badminton seriously, you need to quit everything else and focus solely on this." It's funny how things happen, though.

I never knew there was a Provincial team for girls' soccer. I only found out because I saw someone wearing this cool British Columbia Soccer jacket, and I wanted one. That was how I ended up trying out for the B.C. team and making it. I always tell kids it isn't about the swag, but I guess that jacket, in certain ways, changed the course of my life. It was at the nationals playing for B.C. where I got scouted for the first time and invited into a Women's National Soccer Team training camp. I have to laugh, though. The jacket they handed out to our team turned out to be really ugly. Maybe that's when my brief affair with swag ended. I promise it hasn't been about the gear since.

At the National Team camp, everything changed. I was exposed

to a psychological pressure that I'd never felt before. The coaches used training methodologies that were physically harsh and at times abusive, not to mention demanding. I wasn't sure what to make of it all. Like my badminton coach, this coach also told me I would have to choose one sport if I was going to make it.

When I was in my first year of university, I was one of the top-ranked U19 badminton players in Canada, but I had also just played my first game with the Canadian Women's National Soccer Team. I was being pulled in two different directions, and I just couldn't decide. So, at 19, I had what felt to me like a mini midlife crisis, and I veered off in a totally different direction. I'd heard about an organization called S.A.L.T.S., which stands for Sail and Life

Training Society. It was this grand adventure, spending a year as part of the crew for a tall ship called The Pacific Swift that sailed around the world. It sounded so majestic and beautiful. I had no experience sailing, but I felt called toward it. Maybe I just needed a break because I couldn't choose between badminton and soccer.

Photo credit: Mim Wickett

This experience also proved to be intense, partly because the head cook unfortunately got sick, and I was asked to be one of the new co-head cooks. I had briefly been an assistant cook at a summer camp where I cut carrot sticks and mixed peach drink when I was younger, so perhaps under the circumstances, this qualified me for the this role. But my summer of chopping veggies did not prepare me in any way for what turned out to be a massive undertaking! The good news was that working in the galley left me no time to think about either sport, because my shift often ran from 5 a.m. until 1 a.m. the next day. I had to get provisions and set things up for my co-cook, and then there was the intensity of actually preparing four meals a day for a group of 30 people. And, of course, I got seasick, too. It was extreme, and through it I learned a lot. We sailed from the west coast of North America through the Panama Canal, around Central America, and up through the Caribbean to Miami. Then we went down to St. Lucia and back until we came to the Dominican Republic.

At this stop, my friend and crewmate, Stephen, and I rented motorcycles to visit a remote beach. But the roads at the time in the Dominican Republic frequently transitioned from concrete to gravel and then back to concrete again. They were bad, bumpy and had huge potholes. I was sitting behind Stephen as we came across one of those transitions. We lost control of the motorcycle as the steering jammed, and we ended up crashing hard. We were wearing sandals, shorts, and tank tops and had no helmets on. We were incredibly fortunate it wasn't any worse. I had a road rash up and down the whole right side of my body, and the muffler landed on my calf, burning it. Worst of all, my knee was split open from one edge of it to the other. Stephen had some cuts and road rash and seemed physically okay, but I know it must have been hard for him to see me so torn up.

Locals from the community came by with a pickup truck, loaded us up, and took us to a medical center. Unfortunately, they were also taking us in the opposite direction of the ship. My friend and I tried to tell them they were going the wrong way, but we spoke no Spanish, and they spoke no English. Eventually, we ended up at a one-room medical clinic with bars on the windows and kids peering in from the outside. It was as if we were their entertainment. There was blood in the room, and I watched as they bleached the medical tools from the last procedure to be ready to use on me.

It was wild. No one cleaned the wound out properly, not even when the doctor came in and started to stitch, so there was still dirt and gravel in my knee. Now and then, she would stop working and demand more money before continuing. What was I going to do? I would pay her, and she would keep stitching. There was a police officer in the room, but he asked for my gold necklace, not to mention making some inappropriate comments toward me. Eventually, I don't know how, but we managed to get back to The Pacific Swift. I hobbled on board with a lot of assistance, no cast, no crutches, just a lot of pain. It wasn't long before we realized that something was really wrong.

I was flown on a jumper plane to the main city of Santo Domingo with my fellow shipmate, Mim. Mim spent three days in the hospital with me trying to get me out of the country and back home. The doctor in Santo Domingo did put a cast on my leg, but missed the fact that it had become infected. By the time I got back to Vancouver, I was shivering, sweaty, and the smell coming out of the wound was putrid. I had gangrene.

My parents took me straight to Vancouver Hospital, and I was in surgery within an hour. I was incredibly lucky not to lose my leg. I was in the hospital for 10 days during my recovery and finally had a lot of time to think. It's amazing when we have these moments in life how clear everything can become. Often, we need a catalyst in our life to make us appreciate what we have and give us some direction on where we need to go. I'm not saying you should go out and get gangrene if you're not sure about your path in life. But the accident helped me stop and reflect on what was important to me, and I knew then if I recovered that, I wanted to play soccer.

I know it sounds horrific, but injuries are part of an athlete's journey, and the accident that almost cost me my leg wasn't the only one I experienced in my career. I have also torn my ACL and fractured my femur. Each of those took the better part of a year to heal. **While these injuries were painful, those situations also helped me to learn about what was in my control and what was not.**

One of my favorite quotes is, "Perspective is a state of mind." It is the idea that how we see the world is also shaped by what we choose to believe with our hearts and our minds. Every situation we face is what it is, but we also bring ourselves to the situation. While I can't control whether my hip is dislocated or if my ACL is torn, I can control how I choose to respond. That's what I learned from my parents. Do I view this as a tragedy or as a challenge? That's always up to me to decide. **With an open mind and a grateful heart, we can**

transform our outlook on challenges. This isn't about denying the difficulties, but facing them with resilience, understanding, and optimism. And healing where need be, too.

Would I say the day of the accident was a 'bad day'? No, I wouldn't. I also wouldn't say it was a good day because it wasn't a good day. It was the day the accident happened. Often, we label events as bad, but when we look back at them, they give us a chance to learn some incredibly valuable lessons that we needed to learn at that point. **It can be really hard, but it has been within the challenges that life has thrown at me that I found my true north.** If you can stop in those moments and find your heart, the hard times are what wipe away all the noise and clutter and leave you with just you and what matters most. That's why people talk about the eye of the storm. It's about finding yourself at the center of the maelstrom.

I retired from soccer in December 2007. At that point, I'd spent 18 years with the national team, finishing at age 36. I retired from the National Team before an Olympic year, but I knew it was time. The signs were there, like forgetting my boots or needing to warm up for the warm-up. The culture in some circles of the sport also began to wear on me. I wanted to leave on my own terms, and so I did, content with my accomplishments.

Post-retirement, I haven't left the sport entirely. Instead, I ventured into advocacy and coaching, drawing from my experiences to help push for an open and honest conversation about sports in Canada. As an athlete, at times, your viewpoint can be quite narrow. As I transitioned off the field, I began to see a lot more, some deep systemic issues.

Now, I am grateful to work with leaders across various fields to create environments that prioritize growth, devel-

Photo credit: Canada Soccer

opment, community, and safety. To take the approach that sport is about more than just winning games; it's about our development personally and socially, speaking up when you need to and helping to change the environment for the current and next generations of players. I have a child now, and it underscores again for me the necessity of improving the environment for our young ones. I learned a lot as an athlete and then as a technical coach. Now, as an advocate and leadership coach, I want to inspire positive change as well as support people with their own journey of growth and development. I want to help others see how we can create more environments where athletes and people can thrive, the way my parents did for me.

ABOUT ANDREA NEIL

Andrea Neil was the first woman and the third player overall to be inducted into Canada's Sports Hall of Fame for soccer. With a career that included four FIFA World Cups as an athlete and a leader and three years of coaching within the National Team program, Andrea possesses over two decades of international experience as a leadership expert. Her journey has been enriched by advanced studies in coaching

Photo credit: Ray Shum / Tempest Photo

and leadership in Italy and Holland, contributing to her profound understanding of elite performance. Yet her legacy extends beyond her distinguished athletic achievements. Andrea was a pioneer in women's soccer, helping to light a path for young women in Canada and setting the stage for future generations to follow.

Today, Andrea continues to lead. She integrates her expertise in elite performance, leadership, team building, and psychology from the sports world into the corporate and organizational realm. She firmly advocates that high performance and authentic leadership begin with profound self-awareness, aligning that understanding with a sense of purpose and service. As a subject matter expert in coaching, Andrea's current focus revolves around directing individuals and teams toward high performance interlaced with deeper meaning, inclusion, and safety.

Her presentation topics reflect her commitment to guiding leaders beyond mere outcome goals, encouraging them to embrace a heart-centered vision enriched with deeper values and virtues.

Learn how to navigate life's twists and turns with grace and wisdom in Andrea's powerful message!

REFLECTIONS ON RESILIENCE

Andrea went through an incredibly intense experience and an extremely challenging recovery process after her accident. I truly admire her perspective in not categorizing the incident as a mere bad day. This traumatic event brought about a profound transformation in her mindset, leading to a significant shift in her outlook on life. It acted as a reminder of how short and precious life truly is, offering her the clarity needed to make a pivotal decision regarding her athletic career.

When Andrea made the decision to pursue soccer and successfully returned to the field, she shared a crucial moment with her university coach. He revealed that the team had been struggling over the last year and was in need of a leader.

Despite initially questioning her leadership abilities, considering herself still in the learning phase of the sport of soccer, Andrea's open mind post-accident prompted her to view this as a wonderful opportunity for growth. She recognized the chance to approach things differently and embraced this experiential learning opportunity. Accepting the leadership role, she began by leading herself, ultimately becoming an influential captain on this and several other teams, including the Canadian Women's Soccer National Team.

Think back over your own experiences. Is there an event that happened that you viewed as a "bad" day?

Take a minute and in the space below, briefly write out what happened.

____

____

____

____

____

Next, I challenge you to look at that "bad" moment, event, or day with fresh eyes, considering what you just read in Andrea's story. Was that event a catalyst for you? Did it become a pivotal moment in your life? How did your life change because of that event? Did this event involve another person? If so, imagine looking at the same event from their perspective. How might their viewpoint differ from yours, and how could understanding their perspective influence your response? Write out your reflections in the space below.

____

____

____

____

This exercise might not be easy, but it's a great way to challenge yourself to start looking at situations differently. If we can approach events with a growth mindset, then we realize life isn't happening to us; rather, it is happening *for* us, and we get to choose what we learn and how it can help us going forward.

How can you use what you just learned to help you in the present or in the future? Write it in the space below.

____

____

____

____

____

____

Andrea's story serves as a powerful reminder of the transformative potential inherent in life's challenges. Through her resilience and reflective approach, she redefined her own narrative; this mindset invites us to reconsider our own perspectives on seemingly difficult moments.

When we start to embrace life's challenges as opportunities, we can use them as stepping stones toward growing into and living our very best lives!

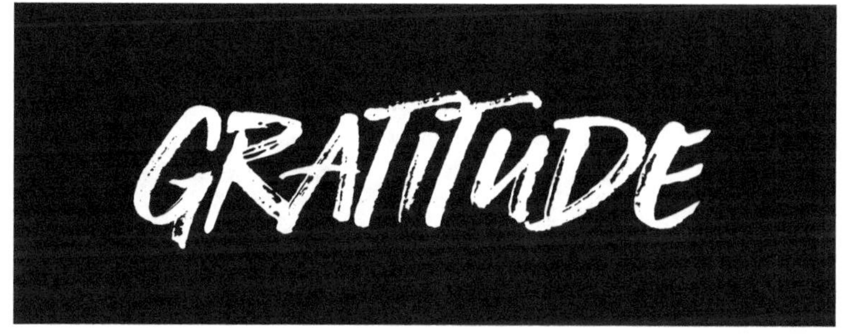
GRATITUDE

CHAPTER 9

Donovan Bailey

DREAM IT. DECLARE IT. DO IT!

Donovan Bailey

I was born in Manchester, Jamaica, and the farm where I grew up overlooked a lush expanse of treetops that often reminded me of the ocean. One of the things I cherished most about where I grew up was the abundance of fruit trees. I loved just plucking an orange or some other fruit from a tree, wiping it off on my shirt, and eating it. I still love the warmth and island vibe of Jamaica. It was a great way for a young boy to grow up. I was 7 years old when I first visited Canada. I moved to Oakville, Ontario, permanently when I was 12. It was quite a shift, from a big island in the Caribbean to a big little town in Canada!

In Jamaica, I was one of the fastest kids on the island. I competed in track and field from a young age, and along with everyone else played cricket and football (soccer). Growing up in Jamaica, netball, similar to basketball, was popular, but only the girls played that. When I got to Canada, I still ran track, but that's where I discovered and then fell in love with basketball.

During my high school years, I played a lot of sports, like volleyball and badminton, in addition to competing in track. I just loved being active. I was extremely competitive. I'm the fourth of five boys in my family, so competition was always there. As I got older and started to compete in track and field, the competitions only fueled the fire. **Being surrounded by the right people and a great coach gave me a competitive edge.**

Throughout high school, I was one of the fastest kids in Canada. However, looking back, I think I was lazy, and took my athleticism for granted. After high school, I took a break from running track and focused on my education and enjoyed playing basketball at Sheridan College, where we won the Canadian championship. It was four years before I competed in track again.

Sometimes people ask me if I just came off the couch to start running again, but during my break from track, I was still playing basketball seven days a week, for as many hours as I could. I stayed in great physical shape. My friends and I played basketball literally all the time; if my parents ever wanted to find me, they'd just look for the nearest basketball court. That's where we would be.

After college, I went to work in corporate Canada, where I became quite successful, but it didn't take long before I was looking for a way out. A few of the athletes I competed against in high school were on the national team, and I had the confident thought that it wouldn't take much for me to beat them again. That is what drew me back to running. Even though I was only 21, I didn't want to lose the window of opportunity to compete. I reconnected with some people I'd met at a national team training camp, and I knew they were serious. Dan Pfaff, my coach, told me I was talented enough to be the best if I could actually focus—a tough thing for a 21-year-old to hear.

So, I moved to Baton Rouge to train with Dan at Louisiana State University. Some of my toughest moments over my athletic career were during practices. I hate practice. I mean, I hate practice. There were so many days where I was convulsing and throwing up everything I'd consumed in the past couple of days because the training was so demanding. Those are some of the days I truly wanted to quit, but I had a goal to reach. There was disappointment when I didn't get selected for a certain team, and deep down I felt I needed to keep going at this because I also didn't want to disappoint my father and hearing him tell me I'm a quitter for the rest of my life! He's never said that, but you get the idea. You know what? There were a lot of days I wanted to quit.

Jumping ahead, another time later in life that I often wanted to quit was during the time I was writing my book, *Undisputed: A Champion's Life*, in 2023. During that journey, I had more than a few days that I thought, "this is crazy!" I had a publisher, but I didn't really understand the commitment and the patience the project would require. To be clear, patience has never been my strong suit! I had to learn it.

As a sprinter, I only had to be patient for 100 meters. But the book was a lot more work than I expected it to be. I'm glad I did it. There were some narratives I wanted to control, but more importantly, I wanted my children to have my story. My daughter was two years old when I became the fastest man in the history of the world, and she will soon turn 30. So, a lot of my drive to make the book as good as it could be motivated my desire to tell the story for my kids. That pulled me through.

One of the things I've done throughout my life is set goals. I started it as a teenager and did it all the way through my athletic career and into my young business career. I still do it today. By doing this, I realize if I don't reach those goals, it's on me. I can't blame anyone else. So, in the

Used with permission from Donovan Bailey

days when I was at practice and the Commonwealth Games or the Olympics were coming up. I knew I was going to prepare and put in the work. I'm not going to be disappointed in myself. Ultimately, you have to be able to pull through those tough days. Taking responsibility for my actions or lack of action was something my parents taught my brothers and me at a young age. I have a strong memory of my parents saying, "Donovan, you've had six months to prepare. Did you? Are you ready? Okay. So, you can't blame someone else."

I learned to respect failure early. As an entrepreneur, I've been both very passive and very aggressive. It's allowed me to win big, and it's allowed me to fail. I am a risk-taker, and I think sports prepares you to be even more so. To me, the word "fail" is indicative of a life lesson. I used those lessons to make sure to eliminate the mistakes I made and then come back stronger. I've developed more of a "win or learn" mentality, as opposed to thinking of "failing" as an endpoint.

One time, I recall my coaches thought I wasn't prepared—well, as least physically prepared—was at the World Championships in Stuttgart in 1993. I knew I was better than some of the guys on our relay team, and mentally I was prepared—but I was relegated to being a substitute. That's the point at which I decided this would never happen again. No one gets to make that decision for me ever again. I vowed to be mentally, physically, psychologically, and financially prepared for anything I take on in the future—sports or business. **I told the coach that this would never happen to me again, and that I would be the world champion, an Olympic champion, and the world record-holder. I just left it there.**

Then, I went to work. I put the blinders on, ignored the noise and chatter around me, and completely focused. There were still some days I wanted to quit, but my goal was precise. When I won the world championships in Sweden, I acknowledged it, but then continued breaking down the race to my coach. I did the same thing after I won the gold medal and broke the world record at the 1996 Olympics in Atlanta. I kept thinking about how terrible my start was and started talking to Dan about it. We went back and forth about it for some time until in the middle of the conversation I said, "I broke the world record!" While I've always been my biggest critic, **I've learned that by consistently evaluating my performance, I can drive myself closer to excellence.**

When I ran in 1997 against Michael Johnson, I had never been that physically prepared for anything. That race was grueling, and I tore my adductor too. I competed for all of 1997 with injuries, but we couldn't tell anyone. I embraced the responsibility of fulfilling my goal. And as the number one athlete in the world, the weight of culture, country, and sports were heavy. So, I chose to grind through the pain. I never counted days competing while injured as any of my worst days. I just got through the pain and got treatment later.

It's all part of being a world-class athlete and a champion. **You get up, get through it,**

Used with permission from Donovan Bailey

and get it done. It's the same story in business. If you want to create greatness, you've got to put in the work. You can always take a nap later.

ABOUT DONOVAN BAILEY

Donovan Bailey is a retired Canadian sports legend who still holds the indoor 50-meter world record. Running track throughout high school, Donovan's sprinting prowess returned in the early 1990s when he transitioned from a career in business administration back to a career competing as a runner at the age of 21.

He set a new world record of 9.84 seconds in the 100 meters at the 1996 Olympic Games in Atlanta, winning Olympic gold.

Apart from individual success, Donovan contributed significantly to Canada's relay teams. His rivalry with American sprinter Michael Johnson had a highlight in a 150-meter race in 1997, which Bailey won, cementing his status as the world's fastest man.

Used with permission from Donovan Bailey

Donovan is the first man to be a world champion, Olympic champion, and world record-holder at the same time. He is the only person to be inducted into Canada's Sports Hall of Fame twice, once as an individual and once as part of the 1996 Summer Olympics team. He was named Sprinter of the Decade (1990s) by *Track and Field News*.

Retiring in 2001, Donovan is an entrepreneur and philanthropist. His book *Undisputed: A Champion's Life* was published in 2023 by Penguin Random House Canada.

Check out this message from Donovan as he shares 3 key tips to help you along your path to success!

REFLECTIONS ON RESILIENCE

Have you ever truly claimed and taken ownership of your goals or dreams? Is there something you desire so intensely that you can taste it, see it, and feel it?

In 1993, Donovan found himself as a substitute on the Canadian men's relay team, as his coaches felt he wasn't physically prepared. Just two years later, he seized gold in the 100m event and the 4x100 relay at the World Championships in Sweden. He then went on to set the 100m world record at Atlanta in 1996 with a time of 9.84 seconds, becoming the world's fastest man. A week later, he anchored the 4x100m relay team to another gold medal. Donovan's remarkable achievements in athletics earned him the prestigious title of Sprinter of the Decade (1990s) by *Track and Field News* and inductions into the Canadian Olympic Hall of Fame, Canada's Sports Hall of Fame, and Canada's Walk of Fame.

What's extremely inspiring is that at the 1993 event, Donovan drew a line in the sand, vowing that he would never again fail to put in the work and allow someone else to dictate his path. He committed himself to preparation and became his own CEO, or as I like to say, the champion of his life. He declared to Coach Mike, "I'll be the world champion. I'll be the Olympic champion. I'll be the world record holder." Once spoken, he knew it was up to him to put in the work, focus, and make it happen.

What some may view as a setback, being a substitute in 1993, became the launchpad for one of the greatest careers in track history.

Even on the toughest days, when quitting seemed tempting, when training pushed him to his limits, and injuries threatened to throw him off course, he remained focused on the pursuit of excellence and the commitment he had made.

This principle of determination and discipline has permeated every aspect of his life. Even amidst the challenges of writing and releasing his book, Donovan persisted, focusing on the end result.

Take a moment now to draw your own line in the sand. What is your burning desire? Write it down. Declare it as boldly as Donovan did to Coach Mike.

____

____

____

Now, close your eyes and immerse yourself in the moment of achieving your goal. Can you visualize it clearly? Picture yourself standing on the podium, accepting an award for your accomplishments in sports, or perhaps you might find yourself smiling as you surpass your health and fitness goals. Picture your name gracing the cover of your bestselling book, or feel the exhilaration of commanding the stage, captivating audiences with your artistic performance or inspiring talk. See your business thriving, providing meaningful impact in the marketplace, or witness the lives being changed by the charity you've passionately founded. Describe this moment in vivid detail—what do you see? How do you feel? Embrace this vision as if it's unfolding before you in the present moment. Write it in the space below.

____

____

____

____

____

____

____

____

____

Now, it is time to take action. It is time to put the blinders on and, as Donovan said, you have to put in the work! There will be days when you will feel discouraged and want to quit. Those are the days to focus on your goal and the commitment you are making to yourself right now. Your determination to your goal will pull you through on the tough days. Remember, greatness takes time, and not all goals manifest as quickly as we would like. It's important to be patient and stay disciplined in doing the right activities. Find a trusted coach, mentor, or friend who you can share your goal with. Speak your dream into existence, put in the work, and watch how you will grow into the champion of your own life.

The world is waiting for you to shine—embrace the journey and make it extraordinary!

DETERMINATION

CHAPTER 10

WHEN THE TIMING IS RIGHT

Moving Forward for Success

WHEN THE TIMING IS RIGHT
Moving Forward for Success

When you first heard the title of this book and while reading through the stories, you may have been thinking, "Phebe, are you saying I never can 'quit' something?" No, I'm not saying that at all. When you know a goal, a dream, a career, a relationship, a lifestyle choice, isn't serving you, your purpose or in alignment with your vision for your future then it may be time to make a change and move forward toward something else. What I am saying by "Never Quit on a Bad Day" is to make that decision on a "good day."

Why a good day? Because if you can transition away from something on a good day, then you are making the decision confidently without all the negative emotions that are typically associated with making a decision on a bad day. You are making that decision because you are looking at your future and realizing that where you are now and what you are doing isn't moving you closer to what you envision for yourself and your future.

WHEN I DECIDED IT WAS TIME TO RETIRE...

It was 2006 and I remember the day vividly when I decided to retire from the Vancouver Whitecaps soccer team. It was very early in pre-season and we had just finished an exhibition game. A new coach had taken over the team. We had a fabulous line up of talent and new players trying out for the upcoming season and we had played a great game. Personally, I was

Photo credit: Vancouver Whitecaps FC / Josh Devins

happy with my performance and knew I had played a good game. The new coach also had a lot of positive feedback for me after the game.

The season before we had finished 3rd in the W-League (the league we played in was called the W-League) and the year before that, we won the W-League Championship. I had so many incredible highs and challenging moments during my career with the Whitecaps.

I still remember my first session with the team like it was yesterday. I had played in Colorado the season before with the Fort Collins Force and as much as I enjoyed the experience, the club, my teammates, I decided that I wanted a chance to play with the incredible players back home who I spent so many years playing against as a youth player. At the time, the team was called the Vancouver Breakers, and the lineup was rock solid, so going into tryouts was nerve-wracking. I remember my excitement when the Coach told me he was signing me to the team, but getting signed was just the first step. Getting signed to a team doesn't necessarily mean playing time. From signing to dressing for games but sitting on the bench, to getting subbed in, to making the starting lineup, to contributing to the team' success, to being awarded W-League Player of the Year, it was a roller coaster of emotions but the one emotion that drove me forward was how much I loved to play soccer, how much I loved playing with my teammates, how much I loved playing in front of my friends and family and how much I loved to compete. I knew that retiring from the Whitecaps didn't mean I would stop any of that. I knew in my heart that I would continue to play soccer, but I also knew that there were other areas of my life that were important to me, and it was time to focus on them.

As I drove home from the game, I was thinking of my future and other goals I had for my life, including my new life as an entrepreneur. As much as I loved playing, I knew that I had other goals that I wanted to accomplish. I pictured what life would look like not playing for the Whitecaps. What life would look like without the many hours of practices, games and time away on road trips. There were many family events that I had missed over the years, and I felt in my heart that it was time. I knew my priorities had shifted.

I took that evening to reflect on the decision that was in my heart. The decision was that it was time. The next day, I let the coach and the club know that I wouldn't be playing in the upcoming season. It wasn't after a bad game or bad practice that I made this decision. I made this decision, as I knew it was best for what I wanted my future to look like. I knew I would continue to play soccer and be involved in the sport (and yes, at the time of publishing this book, I do still play) but I knew that it was time for a shift and transition to focus on other areas of my life. I made that decision and felt a sense of peace mixed with excitement as to what was to come next.

Deciding when to quit or transition can be a challenging and a very tough choice, and there's no one-size-fits-all answer. Here are a few things you may want to consider when making a decision to transition to something new (and remember, make the decision on a good day):

1. If it's not aligned with your values: If what you're doing is in conflict with your personal values, it may be time to transition to something else.

2. If you have achieved what you set out to do: If you've accomplished your goals, it may be time to move onto something new.

3. If you are no longer growing or learning: If you feel like you're no longer developing new skills or knowledge, it may be time to move forward to new opportunities.

4. If you are not making progress despite your focused efforts: If you're putting in significant time and effort, but not seeing any progress or improvement, it may be time to consider a change.

5. If it is affecting your mental or physical health: If what you're doing is causing you significant stress, anxiety, or even physical health problems, it is worth considering whether it may be time to make a change. Be sure to evaluate whether this is just your comfort zone or if it is causing significant emotional anguish.

Transitioning to something new is deeply personal and will depend on your unique situation and future vision. Weighing the pros and cons on a good day and asking a trusted mentor or friend can be helpful too, but it's important to recognize the power of your own instincts and your intuition. Ultimately, it is up to you to determine the best path to creating a fulfilling future.

CHAPTER 11

A CHAMPION'S MINDSET

Success Starts Here!

A CHAMPION'S MINDSET
Success Starts Here!

Throughout the pages of this book, you have read stories from extraordinary individuals who have achieved tremendous success in their athletic and professional careers. By engaging with the Reflections on Resilience sections at the end of each chapter, you've had the opportunity to take note of your own strength and courage. Additionally, you learned powerful strategies to help you push through life's challenging moments.

I genuinely believe that we are all champions. This extends beyond scholastic, athletic, or professional accomplishments; we all have wins that deserve to be celebrated. Each of us possesses the capability to be the champion of our own life.

In my conversations with the featured champions in this book and others I've had the privilege of playing with, learning from, and being inspired by, I'd like to highlight several key attributes of champions for you to reflect on and start or continue to implement along your own journey.

PASSION:

Champions are passionate and enthusiastic about life, their sport, and their goals. They intentionally surround themselves with like-minded individuals. Whether it's in their sport or other endeavors, they choose to surround themselves with positive people who share the same inspiring energy. Champions are aware that their environment can either propel them forward or hinder their progress, so they make deliberate choices.

GRIT:

Champions possess an exceptional level of grit. They are willing to make sacrifices and endure uncomfortable and difficult challenges in pursuit of their goals. Champions finish what they start. They know that true victory is not just about skill or talent; it is about the enduring spirit of resolve that carries them through every trial and tribulation on their journey to the top.

DETERMINATION:

A champion is determined and has a strong sense of purpose. They set clear goals and pursue them with focus. Champions push through hard times by staying focused on their long-term perspective and future vision, even in the face of adversity.

RESILIENCE:

Champions are resilient. They acknowledge that in sports and in life, there will be disappointing moments, setbacks, failures, and challenges. Viewing obstacles as opportunities to learn and grow, champions look to always get better and understand that tough times are temporary. They know that failure is not the opposite of success, but rather a stepping stone toward it.

Champions know if they spend too much time thinking about the last play, they won't be ready for the next one.

ADAPTABILITY:

Champions are flexible and can adapt to changing circumstances. They adjust their strategies, tactics, and approaches, consistently finding ways to succeed. Even when a champion may not "win" the game, they know they have "won" by giving their very best effort.

BELIEF:

Champions believe in themselves, trust in others, and have faith in the process. In challenging times, when a champion's self-belief may waver, they draw strength from the belief of those they trust, fostering a tenacious spirit. Having faith in the process guides champions with an understanding that success often comes through consistent effort and improvement.

CONTINUOUS LEARNING:

Champions recognize the importance of continual growth for success. They actively engage in self-reflection, learn from experiences, and remain dedicated to staying competitive at the top of their game.

DISCIPLINE:

Champions understand that discipline is the foundation for success. They pursue excellence in everything they do, maintaining consistent habits, and demonstrating delayed gratification. Discipline allows them to stay focused on their priorities and goals, and give it their all, even when no one is watching.

POSITIVE MINDSET:

Champions maintain a positive and optimistic outlook. They perceive opportunities in challenges, focus on solutions, and nurture a positive mindset that supports their creativity and success. Positivity is contagious and helps in building strong relationships.

Remember, attitudes are contagious. Is yours worth catching?

LEADERSHIP:

Champions aim to inspire and motivate others. They understand that to lead effectively, they must first be able to lead themselves. Champions have learned when to follow and when to lead. Champions understand the importance of integrity and let their actions speak louder than their words.

HUMILITY:

True champions are humble and open to feedback. They recognize there is always room for improvement and are open and willing to learn from others.

Champions understand that being humble helps maintain healthy relationships and creates a collaborative environment where they and others can thrive.

GRATITUDE:

Champions appreciate others for their efforts and contributions, recognizing the role everyone plays in their success. Even during tough moments, champions are grateful for the journey. Champions express gratitude, understanding that gratitude helps shift emotions and uplifts both the recipient and the giver.

Remember, the journey to becoming and staying a champion is a continual process. You may not be where you want to be, but celebrate the progress you are making. Be intentional every day about growing into the champion you were born to be, go after your dreams with excitement, and always remember...

THANK YOU!

Hi Friend,

You are an amazing and ambitious person who looks to make the most out of life, and I am thankful for who you are and the positive impact you will make on your community. The fact that you purchased this book and made it to this page shows your determination and drive. You have the potential and ability to turn your dreams into a beautiful reality.

I have been inspired by many individuals along my journey, and I wanted to create something that would encourage others as well.

Partial proceeds from all Never Quit on a Bad Day books and merchandise sales will go to Right to Play, as I believe sports/play is such a powerful vehicle for children to learn, grow, and develop, and to the Canadian Cancer Society. I lost my dad to cancer in 2012, causing some of the toughest days of my life.

Thank you for making a positive difference in the lives of others by being a part of and supporting the Never Quit on a Bad Day series.

Wishing you continued success,

KEEP YOUR COMMITMENT IN SIGHT

Are you focused on accomplishing a goal or big dream? Are you determined to push through your challenging days? Are you excited about your future?

Keep your commitment to your goals and dreams visible with a daily reminder.

Join the Never Quit on a Bad Day Community

NEVER QUIT ON A BAD DAY™

Inspiring Stories of Resilience

THRIVING ENTREPRENEURS EDITION

- Gain insight by learning from successful entrepreneurs
- Know you are not alone in your struggles – we all have bad days
- Acquire new tools to help you persevere through challenges in your life
- Learn from Phebe how to have a winning mindset
- Discover your capacity for greatness and how to tap into it

Available on Amazon

SCAN THE QR CODE

Get Social & You May Be Featured as Our Never Quit on a Bad Day Enthusiast of the Month!

Inspire yourself and others to stay on track by sharing your Never Quit on a Bad Day commitment. Take a picture holding or wearing your 'Never Quit on a Bad Day' book, accessories, and/or clothing. Post the picture along with one of your goals on social media, and please tag us **@NeverQuitOnABadDay** and include the hashtag **#NeverQuitOnABadDay**. Every month, we will select one person to be featured on social media as our Never Quit on a Bad Day Enthusiast of the Month.

Together, let's create a ripple of positive change by encouraging others to commit to their goals and join Never Quit on a Bad Day community too!

LET'S CONNECT!

www.NeverQuitOnABadDay.com
IG: @NeverQuitOnABadDay
FB: NeverQuitOnABadDay

Sign up and join the Never Quit on a Bad Day community. Be the first to know about our next book release in the *Never Quit on a Bad Day* series, plus receive other insider perks too!

ABOUT PHEBE TROTMAN

Phebe Trotman is a successful and heart-centered entrepreneur based in Vancouver, Canada, who is passionate about helping others discover their joy. In both her athletic and professional careers, Phebe's personal success has been a testament that anything is possible with hard work, dedication, and a team-centered approach.

As an athlete, Phebe made a name for herself in the soccer world, achieving numerous awards and accolades. She has been inducted into the Coquitlam Sports Hall of Fame as an athlete, been honored as a team member in the BC Sports Hall of Fame and Museum, and recognized on two teams in the Burnaby Sports Hall of Fame. She is also listed on the BC Soccer Heritage Roll of Honour and holds several titles such as two-time Master's National Champion, W-League Champion, W-League Player of the Year, Women's Premier League National Champion, Simon Fraser University Female Athlete of the Year, NAIA Champion, NAIA Championship finals MVP, NAIA Women's Soccer Player of the Year, two-time First Team All-American, and Under-19 National Champion.

Phebe is committed to promoting the game of soccer. She is actively shaping its future through her coaching and mentorship of the next generation of players and coaches. Since 2009, Phebe has been leading the Coquitlam Metro-Ford Soccer Club Initiation Program for players aged three to seven years old. This program emphasizes skill development, physical literacy, and the improvement of psychomotor and cognitive skills, which prepare young players for success in the sport and in life.

In the business world, Phebe's drive and dedication propelled her to the top rank in her network marketing company. Phebe has received numerous company awards, including recognition as the Top International Customer Sponsor, Global Trainer of the Year, Runner Up Global Distributor of the Year, and Global Distributor of the Year. She has also been featured in magazines such as *Success From Home* and *Networking Times*, as well as on the #1 Global Podcast "MLM Nation" and in the book, *The Four Year Career for Women*.

Phebe is a champion for personal growth and believes that reaching one's full potential creates a ripple effect of inspiration and motivation. Phebe is passionate about helping others on their own journeys to unlocking their potential and living their best lives. With her dedication to empowering others, Phebe is a powerful force for positive change.

SPEAKING AND TRAINING

Looking for a keynote speaker and trainer who can deliver a powerful and inspiring message at your next event?

Phebe Trotman is an engaging and dynamic communicator and coach who is passionate about helping individuals and teams achieve their fullest potential. She combines her unique perspective and wealth of experience in network marketing, athletics, and team-centered coaching to offer practical insights

Photo credit: Kanopi Creative

and strategies for success in an entertaining presentation style that can help your team or audience excel, both personally and professionally.

Whether you're organizing a small workshop, a corporate or team building event, or company convention, Phebe has the skills and expertise to deliver a presentation that will resonate with your audience and leave a lasting impact.

Her friendly and approachable manner makes her a great choice for events of all sizes, and she is dedicated to making every event an unforgettable experience for your audience or team.

So, if you're looking for a keynote speaker who can help you take your event to the next level, think of Phebe Trotman. She will create a presentation that will inspire, inform, and motivate your audience to achieve their fullest potential.

www.NeverQuitOnABadDay.com

Photo credit: Kanopi Creative

WITH HEARTFELT APPRECIATION

To my wonderful *Never Quit on a Bad Day*™ - *Accomplished Athletes* contributors: Carl Valentine, Dante Fabbro, Joel Anthony, Dr. John Frank, Julia Budd, Ronnie Jagday, Scott Morgan, Jason Holder, Andrea Neil and Donovan Bailey. Thank you for saying yes! Your commitment to excellence, along with your determination, hard work and humility truly marks you as champions through and through. This book stands as a testament to your dedication, showcasing the exceptional stories of individuals who have not only achieved greatness in their athletic pursuits but have also become a bright light of inspiration for others. Without your commitment to your goals and dreams, this endeavor would not have been possible. I want to express my heartfelt appreciation for sharing your stories. Your openness has added depth and authenticity to this book, making it a powerful tribute to the spirit of triumph over adversity. I look forward to seeing the ripple effect of your influence on those who will read these pages. As we celebrate your accomplishments, I am honored to call you friends. I am forever grateful for the privilege of capturing and sharing your extraordinary journeys.

To my parents, Henderson and Joyce. Mom and Dad, your love and guidance have been the foundation of my life, and I am eternally thankful for the sacrifices you made to help me become the person I am today. Dad, although you may be in Heaven, I can hear you very (very) loudly cheering me on during the writing and release of this book. Thank you for always being my biggest champion. Mom, I'm so grateful for you. Your constant prayers, support and belief gives me the confidence to dream big and always pursue my life's passions.

To my brother TeRoi and Chanda, thanks for always inspiring me to be the best I can be in whatever I do in life; to take risks and to live a fun-filled adventurous life! Chanda, you are an incredible mother and I'm so thankful that I have a sister now too! I really appreciate all your support over the years. Skylar and Tatum, thanks for being the best nieces ever and helping me choose the background music for the book videos.

To the Trotman, Springer, Belgrave, Ewers, Ryan, Parsons, Watkins, Hunt, Lowe, Parkins, Sutherland, Branch, Clarke, Morrison, Wellington, and Thunstrom families - you are simply the BEST! I am so thankful to have such a supportive and loving family who lead by example in caring for each other and loving others. Your support, love, and guidance have been key in helping me achieve my goals, and I feel blessed to have you all in my life.

Kori and Steven, thank you both for your continuous encouragement, support, mentorship, leadership, and prayers. Throughout our years of friendship, we have shared numerous exceptional experiences, and I believe we are just getting started. I am grateful for all the insight, wisdom, and love you have shown me. Sissy, your encouragement and guidance have been essential on my journey, and I am truly grateful for your presence in my life.

Vanessa, from the moment I shared the vision for this book series with you, you have been a constant source of encouragement. Your belief in me and the vision for this book series has been instrumental in making this book series become a reality. Thank you for the beautiful foreword and afterword you wrote for the *Thriving Entrepreneurs* book. Your words set the perfect tone for the book. Thank you for your incredible friendship and mentorship throughout the years.

Virgil, thank you for being an incredible supporter throughout the process of writing this book series. From the very first chat with you about my idea for this book series, you have encouraged me and stood in my corner cheering for me. You have been by my side through every step, from the first look at book cover drafts, to the evolution of the logo, to the collection of stories and now, this next finished book. Your love has been a true source of strength for me. Your belief in me and this book series has meant the world to me, and I am beyond grateful to have you in my life.

To my friends who are like family: Karlan, Ellice and Patrick, Sadie and Mark, Jenn, Jessie, Benny, Monique, Jameila, Sarah, Osita, Tanya, Shawndra, Renita, Natasha, Darron, Dowan, Modi, Danny, Kyla and Antonio, Duette, Casey, Michelle, KJ, Lisa, Ivan, Efe and Tom, you all are my tribe. I am truly blessed to have such outstanding people like you all in my life. Thanks for always keeping it real and being there through thick and thin. Your love and laughter over the years has lifted me up even during the hardest times of my life, and you always know how to make the good times even better. I cherish each and every one of you and feel incredibly grateful to have such an amazing group of friends in my life.

Kwame, thank you for the incredible impact you have had on my life. Your recommendation to read *Rich Dad, Poor Dad* was a catalyst that set me on my entrepreneurial journey, and I am forever grateful for your guidance and encouragement over the years.

Mike and Darren, thank you for the extra gentle nudge (smile). It was through that impactful conversation that the seed for this book series was first planted.

To my book designers, Margaret and Blake of Margaret Cogswell Designs, thank you for bringing my vision to life with your talent and creativity. Your ability to capture the essence of my message through your designs have been truly remarkable. It has been a pleasure collaborating with you, and I want you to know how grateful I am to you for your dedication to this book series.

To my editor, Melody of Publishing Concierge, working with you on this book series continues to be a lovely experience. From our very first conversation to the final moments of completing this second book in the series, your support and insightful feedback have been invaluable. Your guidance has been essential in shaping this book series. I am grateful for you, your hard work and your incredible skill.

To my proofreader, Julie of Creative Curvy Services, thank you for your attention to detail and suggestions as we worked together to create a polished final product.

To my brand strategist, Byron of Coastlines Creative Group, thank you for your hard work and dedication in creating an impressive logo to represent the essence of Never Quit on a Bad Day. I appreciate the time and research you put into this project.

To my website team, Sandro and Kelsey of Stigan Media, and Laura and the team at Virtual Squirrel Business Support Services, your skills and expertises have helped me to create a beautiful and professional online presence. Your creativity and passion shine through in all that you do.

To my incredible *Never Quit on a Bad Day™ - Thriving Entrepreneurs* contributors: Jordan Adler, Jimmy Dick, Mike Dreher, Darren Ewert, Jen Furness, Jeanie Fountain, Steve Schulz, Dave and Roxanne Obiso, Scott Pospichal and Simon Chan. Thank you for saying yes and sharing your inspiring story. Your story of resilience is continuing to inspire people around the world to pursue their goals passionately.

To my wonderful Alpha team: Michelle, Ivan, Renita, Sarah W., Liam, Sandi, Sophie, Nadia, Sarah T., Paulo, Eddie, Lindsay, and Ricardo, thank you for saying yes and your willingness to help. I asked each of you because of the tremendous respect I have for you and the support you have provided over the years. I appreciate your feedback and I am grateful to have you on my Alpha team and, more importantly, in my life.

To my Never Quit on a Bad Day Community and its future members, I appreciate you and your continuous support. Keep chasing those dreams and reaching for those goals – I am cheering you on every step of the way!

To the CMFSC Technical Team: Sara, Alfredo, Andrea, Liam, Lindsay, Michelle, Esteban, Dale and Rob; Alex and the CMFSC Board; Rae; Neil and Initiation Program Staff Coaches, I feel incredibly fortunate to be part of a coaching crew that is so dedicated and passionate about soccer. Your enthusiasm and commitment to helping young players develop and grow both on and off the field is truly inspiring. I have learned so much from each of you, and it is an honor to work alongside such talented and dedicated coaches.

To Cory, Erin, Jen, Kristen, and my Coquitlam FBBC Family, thank you for pushing me to my limits and inspiring me to be the best version of myself. Your dedication to health and wellness has been a constant reminder of the importance of taking care of ourselves both physically and mentally.

To my soccer teammates, past and present, as I look back on my many years of playing soccer, my heart is filled with appreciation as I remember all the incredible lifelong friendships I have made through this sport. From the celebrations and laughter to the heartbreak and even tears, we have shared so many moments together. I want to express my deep gratitude for always inspiring me to work hard both on and off the field. Your commitment to working hard and achieving our goals as a team has taught me valuable lessons about teamwork and dedication. I am grateful for the many lessons I have learned from each and every one of you over the years.

To my soccer coaches, throughout my life, I have been fortunate to have had many coaches who have taught me invaluable lessons about leadership, inspiration, and teamwork. From my childhood to now, each coach has imparted their unique wisdom, helping me to better understand how to motivate and unite a team to work towards a shared goal. I am grateful for the lessons I have learned from each of you, as these have helped shape me into the leader I am today. Thank you for all that you have taught me over the years, and for instilling in me the values of hard work, integrity, and dedication.

To Ps. Durwin; Ps. Troy and Rachel; Ps. Shane and Rachel (and the Resonate family), your unwavering faith has been a constant source of inspiration, and thank you for reaching out to connect at times when I've always needed it the most.

Kody B. and Jodi, thank you for creating a phenomenal movement that I'm honored to be associated with. Over the years, I have learned so much from both of you. You have taught me the immense power of acting on promptings and how we can change not only our own life but the lives of others as well.

Team Legacy and Team Impact, you are all simply amazing! As I think of all the team members, past and present, who have said 'yes', my heart fills with gratitude. Your dedication and passion for pursuing your dreams are truly inspiring. We have shared so many fantastic moments and watching you all achieve great things in your lives fuels my own determination to keep pushing forward. I love seeing you all shining in your own unique ways, and I want you to know that I will always be your biggest cheerleader, rooting for you in everything you do.

Dave O., thank you for knowing that SOC was for me before I knew it was for me.

To the fabulous SOC Corporate Executive Team, SOC Customer Success Team: Walter, Sandra, Kathy, Jen, John and team, my fellow Eagles: Jordan, Bob and BettyAnn, Diane, Melissa and the incredible SOC field leaders: Dave and Lori, Callie, Gayle and Steve, Judy, Willie, Shawn, Joy, April, Dhea, and the SOC affiliates

- past and present, you are a group of truly exceptional people. I'm continually inspired by you and your dedication to positively changing lives with the message of promptings. I have learned so much from you all over the years. You all have such big hearts and I'm honored to be a part of such a supportive and uplifting community.

To my BNI Marinaside Family, I feel like I've grown up in business with you all. I'll be forever grateful for the impact you have had on me personally and professionally. I could not have made it this far as an entrepreneur without your support and guidance.

To you, the reader, again I want to express my sincerest gratitude for taking the time to read this book. I pray that the stories and insights shared throughout, along with the Reflections on Resilience exercises, have provided you with the empowerment and encouragement needed to persevere through tough times. Remember, your dreams are within your reach, go after them with passion and confidence, and **Never Quit on a Bad Day!**

WORDS OF PRAISE
What Readers Are Saying

Must Read! ⭐⭐⭐⭐⭐

Loved how this book was set up with easy to read stories and reflection exercises that can be read cover to cover or modularly. Each testimony was well captured; personal with purpose. As someone who can lack the time and focus to read, I found these burst of inspiration just what I needed! Thank you Phebe!! Looking forward to the series to come.

-Lynn

A must read for all dreamers. ⭐⭐⭐⭐⭐

Never Quit on a Bad Day is an uplifting look at how to conquer the obstacles that stand in the way of your ultimate goal. I loved that it didn't just make me think about my own goals but how I support those around me and what role am I playing to them. Each story is short but impactful with a beautiful and easy to connect with message (even though I've never flown a helicopter). This book will undoubtedly have a positive impact on your life and those around you.

-Amazon Customer

Inspiring!! ⭐⭐⭐⭐⭐

In "Never Quit on a Bad Day," Phebe's enduring inspiration translates seamlessly onto the pages. Her book is a heartfelt invitation to embrace resilience, providing relatable short stories, engaging exercises, and actionable wisdom that resonate deeply. "Never Quit on a Bad Day" equips us with the tools to not only face adversity, but to thrive within it. So, grab a cup of tea, a pen, and paper, and allow this book to empower you on your journey of personal growth.

-Sydney

Fantastic self improvement book! ⭐⭐⭐⭐⭐

If you are looking for a well thought out and simple to follow guide to navigate the waters of personal growth and self improvement, this book is it! The book is packed with a wealth of information, with personal experience stories, which makes it an easy and enjoyable read.

-happy customer

Very relatable and empowering.

This book is a great reminder that after every storm comes another sunny day filled with opportunities. What I appreciated most about this book is its practicality. Thank you for sharing your stories and motivating words.

It's a must-read that will leave you feeling motivated and ready to face life's challenges head-on. Well done!

-Amazon Customer

Loved the reflection sections, found them helpful

I loved the Reflections on Resilience sections at the end of each chapter. These thought-provoking questions served as a source of inspiration, encouraging me to persevere through a bit of a life rough patch. It's a powerful addition that adds both depth and practical encouragement to the book.

-K Mobilio

Beautifully Inspiring Stories

After only a few chapters in, this book definitely inspires! Beautiful stories of real people (including the author!) of pushing through adversity and coming out the other side, when things aren't necessarily looking so great or you're feeling defeated. Would recommend to anyone and everyone.

-PP

WOW!! A great and inspiring read!

I don't write many reviews but when something really inspires me - I have to shout it from the rooftops! This book should be assigned reading in high school and beyond. Such inspirational stories that really resonated with me. There are so many relatable stories that I can apply to my life. Thank you, Phebe, for bringing this collection together as well as filling it with practical advice that can be applied to any situation. Everyone can benefit from this book - I highly recommend it.

-C. Peterson

Keep this close at hand

I love this book for a number of reasons. It is easy to pick up, especially on a bad day, to remind oneself to get back up and keep going. It is ideal for grabbing when you have a few minutes to read, and it also has some blanks for the reader to fill in as reminders and to help a person change. The format helps you see examples of people from all backgrounds, and how they overcame and continue to overcome challenges.

This is a book to keep close at hand for a pick-me-up, reference, and source of inspiration. Highly recommend this book as a resilience builder to people in all walks of life.

-J. Kennel

Everyone should read this book!!!

What a book of hope & inspiration. With tears streaming down my face I enjoyed every word!

-Sondra K.

I couldn't put it down

Such a great read! Great stories of overcoming adversities through faith & resilience. The lessons teach us at getting good failing forward until we figure it out. That is what people need to understand and get OK with. I will read this book again & again as a reminder that life will keep knocking us down when we least expect it & it's how we respond to those lessons that will determine the trajectory of our lives.

-Bryan

We would LOVE to hear from you!

Please take a moment to share your thoughts in an honest review, as your feedback is greatly appreciated.

www.NeverQuitOnABadDay.com/Review

www.ingramcontent.com/pod-product-compliance
Lightning Source LLC
Chambersburg PA
CBHW051106050726
47592CB00002B/698